TORAH AND THE CHRONICLER'S HISTORY WORK
An Inquiry into the Chronicler's References to Laws, Festivals, and Cultic Institutions in Relationship to Pentateuchal Legislation

Program in Judaic Studies
Brown University
BROWN JUDAIC STUDIES
Edited by
Jacob Neusner
Wendell S. Dietrich, Ernest S. Frerichs, William Scott Green,
Calvin Goldscheider, David Hirsch, Alan Zuckerman

Project Editors (Projects)

David Blumenthal, Emory University (Approaches to Medieval Judaism)
William Brinner (Studies in Judaism and Islam)
Ernest S. Frerichs, Brown University (Dissertations and Monographs)
Lenn Evan Goodman, University of Hawaii (Studies in Medieval Judaism)
William Scott Green, University of Rochester (Approaches to Ancient Judaism)
Norbert Samuelson, Temple University (Jewish Philosophy)
Jonathan Z. Smith, University of Chicago (Studia Philonica)

Number 196
TORAH AND THE CHRONICLER'S WORK
An Inquiry into the Chronicler's References to Laws, Festivals, and
Cultic Institutions in Relationship to Pentateuchal Legislation

by
Judson R. Shaver

TORAH AND THE CHRONICLER'S HISTORY WORK
An Inquiry into the Chronicler's References to Laws, Festivals, and Cultic Institutions in Relationship to Pentateuchal Legislation

by

Judson R. Shaver

Scholars Press
Atlanta, Georgia

TORAH AND THE CHRONICLER'S HISTORY WORK
An Inquiry into the Chronicler's References to Laws, Festivals, and Cultic Institutions in Relationship to Pentateuchal Legislation

© 1989
Brown University

Library of Congress Cataloging in Publication Data

Shaver, Judson Rayford.
   Torah and the Chronicler's history work : an inquiry into the
Chronicler's references to laws, festivals, and cultic institutions
in relationship to pentateuchal legislation / by Judson R. Shaver.
   p.   cm. -- (Brown Judaic studies ; no. 196)
   Includes bibliographical references.
   ISBN 1-55540-417-0
   1. Bible. O.T. Chronicles--Relation to the Pentateuch.
2. Bible. O.T. Pentateuch--Relation to Chronicles. I. Title.
II. Series.
BS1345.5.S48 1989
222'.606--dc20
                                      89-24041
                                      CIP

ISBN 978-1-930675-37-7 (alk. paper : paper)

Printed in the United States of America
on acid-free paper

∞

FOR PAGE

She is far more precious than pearls.
Prov. 31:10

Contents

Preface

This book originated in Professor Joseph Blenkinsopp's Second Temple Seminars in the late 1970s at the University of Notre Dame, where it was submitted in penultimate form as a doctoral dissertation in October 1983. I am indebted to many, but especially to Dr. Blenkinsopp, who directed the dissertation and was a constant source of insight and inspiration. With gratitude and fond memories, I also acknowledge the Danforth Foundation, whose support made possible my doctoral studies, and the James Still Fellowship Program of the Applachian Center at the University of Kentucky, where I was provided the time and space to finish my dissertation.

Despite the number of years since the dissertation was completed, I have been encouraged to publish this book by Professor Ralph Klein, the Chair, and others of my colleagues in the Chronicles, Ezra, Nehemiah Group of the *Society of Biblical Literature*,[1] and from Professor Jacob Neusner, whose support of younger scholars is generous and well known. I wish also to express my appreciation to Dr. David Pollick, formerly the Dean of the College of Arts and Sciences at Seattle University, for his support of this project, and to Ms. Bonita Kroon, whose word processing skills proved essential.

I wish also to thank the many friends and colleagues who have in their own ways provided the help I needed in the process of writing this book. I am indebted especially, however, to my children, Nathan and Sarah, for the joy they add to my life, and to

---

[1] A number of important works bearing on the topic have been published since the completion of the dissertation. See especially, Michael Fishbane, *Biblical Interpretation in Ancient Israel* (Oxford, 1985); H.G.M. Williamson, *Ezra-Nehemiah* (Waco, 1985); Roddy L. Braun, *1 Chronicles* (Waco, 1986); Raymond B. Dillard, *2 Chronicles* (Waco, 1987); and Joseph Blenkinsopp, *Ezra-Nehemiah: A Commentary* (Philadelphia, 1988).

my friend and colleague, Professor James Parry, whose generous interest in my work played an important role in the making of this book. Finally, I wish to thank my wife, Page Shaver, for her encouragement and unflagging support. In appreciation, this is dedicated to her.

Judson R. Shaver

Seattle University
Seattle, Washington
July 25, 1989

Abbreviations

Ant.	Josephus, *Jewish Antiquities*
AP	Aramaic Papyri published in Cowley, A. *Aramaic Papyri of the Fifth Century B.C.* Oxford: Clarendon Press, 1923.
BZAW	Beiheft zur *Zeitschrift für die alttestamentliche Wissenschaft*, Berlin
CBQ	*The Catholic Biblical Quarterly*, Washington
Ev.	English version
HTR	*Harvard Theological Review*, Cambridge, Mass.
JBL	*Journal of Biblical Literature*, Atlanta
JTS	*Journal of Theological Studies*, Oxford
MT	Masoretic text
RSV	Revised Standard Version
VT	*Vetus Testamentum*, Leiden
ZAW	*Zeitschrift für die alttestamentliche Wissenschaft*, Berlin

Chapter 1

Introduction

The study of the Hebrew Bible in the modern period has been greatly influenced by the powerful analytical tools forged by post-enlightenment thinkers. These research tools or methods, literary-, source-, form-, and tradition-criticism, coupled with a new historiography, produced the invaluable approach known as the historical-critical method.

It is hardly necessary to rehearse the ways in which this new approach has enhanced our understanding of Hebrew Bible texts. Yet like all strong medicine the new methods had unforeseen and sometimes debilitating side effects. A clear understanding of the human provenance of the Hebrew Bible has for many raised the question of the authority of scripture or canon. On the other hand, the careful cross-examination of individual sources and traditions has tended toward an atomization of the biblical witness and an inflated valuation of original or earlier texts at the expense of the canonical redaction.

The recognition of these shortcomings prompted several new kinds of research all of which are sometimes called canon criticism. A work such as Coats and Long's *Canon and Authority* is representative of a growing literature of response to the theological challenge regarding the authority of the canon,[1] while Childs' interest is primarily in Biblical Theology and thus in exegesis in a canonical context.[2] A related, but different, enterprise represented

---

[1] George W. Coats and Burke O. Long (eds.), *Canon and Authority* (Philadelphia, 1977).
[2] Brevard S. Childs, *Biblical Theology in Crisis* (Philadelphia, 1970).

by Sanders and Blenkinsopp has a more historical objective.[3]   That is, rather than addressing specifically theological questions such as the authority of the Hebrew Bible in the church or issues like the theology of the canon, such research attempts to account for the religious, political and social factors which contributed to the formation of the Hebrew canon. This approach, far from being an attempt to resort to the pre-critical past, is rigorous in its historical-critical methodology. It faults prior criticism, which analyzed the historical context or milieu of biblical traditions at every stage of development except the last, only for not following its own insights and methods far enough. Such canon criticism insists that an understanding of the last stage, the canonical, is a necessary part of the interpretative framework. The present research is of this latter type and is intended to clarify one facet of the larger problem of reconstructing the historical events and editorial activities that produced the final stages in the formation of the Torah canon.

It has been a century since Julius Wellhausen published his epoch-making *Prolegomena zur Geschichte Israels*, in which he concluded that the priestly legislation was not prior but subsequent to the vital period of classical prophecy, that the Mosaic legislation stands not at the fount of ancient Israel but rather at the origins of Judaism in the Second Temple period.[4]   These conclusions were based in part on a remarkably thorough analysis and comparison of hexateuchal legal and narrative traditions which disclosed four basic source documents and a final redactor. In order of their antiquity they are the Jehovistic history-book (JE), the "book of the Torah" (D), the Holiness Code (H), and the Priestly Code (RQ) made up of an independent document (Q - *Quelle*) and the redactional elements of the final priestly revision of the Hexateuch (R).

According to Wellhausen, JE extends from the account of creation through the conquest of Canaan. While E, whatever its original form, was preserved in fragments which cannot usefully be separated from J, the combined narrative dates from the Golden Age of the Davidic--Solomonic Empire. In his analysis of D Wellhausen depended on de Wette, who had shown that D was "the book of the

---

[3] James Sanders, *Torah and Canon* (Philadelphia, 1972); Joseph Blenkinsopp, *Prophecy and Canon* (Notre Dame and London, 1977).

[4] Julius Wellhausen, *Prolegomena to the History of Israel*, trans. Menzies and Black (New York, 1957). The work was first published in 1878; a second edition was published in 1883 with the new title *Prolegomena zur Geschichte Israels*.

law" mentioned in 2 Kgs. 22:8 and discovered in 621 B.C.E. Wellhausen went beyond de Wette, however, and argued that D was in fact the law of Israel from the day in 621 on which Josiah had it publicly read through the exile until it was finally replaced by the Pentateuch in the time of Ezra. The Holiness Code (Lev. 17-26) was an exilic product of a "school" founded by Ezekiel; RQ was the same school's later product. This latter was composed of an independent stem which Wellhausen termed "The book of origins" (Q - *Quelle*) and those elements attributable to the final priestly redactor of the Hexateuch (R), which consisted of "innumerable additions and supplements [primarily] to Q...but not to it alone, and indeed to the whole of the Hexateuch."[5]

Thus the Hexateuch was made up of JE, D, H and RQ, but because RQ signifies the final redaction of the entire Hexateuch the whole could be referred to as RQ. This was produced in Babylon, and brought by Ezra to Palestine in 458 B.C.E.[6] With the arrival of Nehemiah in 445 B.C.E. conditions permitted Ezra to promulgate the Pentateuch on the first day of the seventh month of 444 B.C.E.[7]

Despite its monumental importance and unparalleled influence on pentateuchal studies, Wellhausen's *Prolegomena* fails at exactly the point of our present interest, namely, the final stages in the formation of the Pentateuch. That is, Wellhausen provides a documentary analysis of the *Hexateuch*; he argues that this *Hexateuch* was produced in Babylon, brought by Ezra to Palestine in 458, and that fourteen years later Ezra published the *Pentateuch*. Wellhausen offers not a word of explanation as to who is responsible for the reduction of the Hexateuch to the Pentateuch or why this reduction occurred.

In addition to this particularly noteworthy lacuna, there are several points in Wellhausen's analysis of the mission of Ezra which need further investigation. Neither the certainty with which Wellhausen dated Ezra's arrival in Palestine nor the date itself is by any means typical of modern scholarship.[8] Further, the longstanding view that Ezra brought the "law of the God of Heaven" with him from Babylon to Palestine is not unambiguously supported by the text of Ezra 7. Indeed, the implication of 7:25 seems to be

---

[5] Wellhausen, *Prolegomena*, p. 385.

[6] Wellhausen, *Prolegomena*, pp. 384-85.

[7] Wellhausen, *Prolegomena*, pp. 405-407.

[8] Cf. below, pp. 20-26.

that this law was already known in Palestine.[9]   Finally, whether Ezra brought the law to Palestine or not, Wellhausen has not demonstrated that what Ezra promulgated was in fact the Pentateuch. That is, even if it is the case, as Wellhausen believes, that the specifics of Ezra's law conform in every way to the stipulations of the Priestly legislation, that does not yet establish that it was the Pentateuch that Ezra published rather than the Hexateuch, or P. Even the correspondence of Ezra's law with the P legislation remains problematic, for while there are undeniable agreements, there is a notable exception. I refer to *Yom Kippur*, the memorial of the fast-days of the exile. Wellhausen pointed out, quite correctly, that it was intercalated into the liturgical calendar by P and was to be celebrated on the tenth day of the seventh month. He does not, however, take any notice of its absence in Neh. 8 which records both the reading of the law on the first day of the seventh month as well as the subsequent liturgical events of that month.[10]   This is all the more surprising since it is precisely the sort of exegetical evidence on which Wellhausen's theory depends. Now clearly the absence of *Yom Kippur* in Neh. 8 does not disprove Wellhausen's thesis; it is, however, a fact which must be accounted for in Wellhausen's or any other theory as to the identity of Ezra's law.

Despite his cultural and philosophical biases (the most important of which were Hegelianism and Romanticism)[11] the rigor of Wellhausen's exegetical method has assured his basic conclusions of broad acceptance which in many cases extends even to their details. That is not to say that the tasks of pentateuchal criticism had all been accomplished, however, although that is apparently the view Wellhausen took, but only that all such criticism since Wellhausen has had to take account of his work and that most of it depends on the *Prolegomena* to a greater or lesser extent.

While Wellhausen turned his energies to other tasks, his successors in pentateuchal studies continued his investigations and

---

[9] Cf. below, pp. 35-36, 73-74.

[10] Cf. Roland de Vaux, *Ancient Israel: Its Life and Institutions*, trans. John McHugh (London, 1961), pp. 509-10.; Morton Smith, *Palestinian Parties and Politics that Shaped the Old Testament* (New York, 1971), pp. 123, 273; Joseph Blenkinsopp, "Interpretation and the Tendency to Sectarianism: An Aspect of Second Temple History," in E.P. Sanders, *et al* . (eds.), *Jewish and Christian Self-Definition, II: Two Aspects of Judaism in the Greco-Roman Period* (Philadelphia, 1981), p. 6.

[11] Cf. Blenkinsopp, *Prophecy and Canon*, pp. 19-22.

elaborated or challenged his theory in significant ways. Some, of course, abandoned it, but others especially in Germany began to develop it into what we may call the new documentary hypothesis.[12] Thus von Rad notes at the beginning of his essay, "The Form-Critical Problem of the Hexateuch," that documentary criticism seems to have reached a dead end, that further research must direct itself toward the present canonical form of the Hexateuch.[13] Von Rad continued to deal with the documents, JEDP, but no longer as if they were the compositions of individual authors that could be precisely dated. Rather the source documents were the final product of a long redactional process which joined units of tradition from a wide range of dates. On the other hand, Martin Noth, in two major studies, *Überlieferungsgeschichtliche Studien I* and *Überlieferungsgeschichte des Pentateuch*, developed his theory that Deuteronomy through 2 Kings is a literary unit, the Deuteronomistic History (Dtr), and that it existed independently of the Tetrateuch.[14] Thus J, E, and P end with the book of Numbers (except for redactional elements in Deut. 31-34), and Deuteronomy belongs properly to the Deuteronomistic History. It follows that there never was a Hexateuch. Regarding the documentary sources of the Tetrateuch, Noth held that P was an independent narrative on which the whole was based, and that J and E were both complete narratives based on a common source, the *Grundlage* (G), which was itself composed by the joining together of five originally independent themes.

It is only in a most general sense that one can speak of a consensus in the field of pentateuchal criticism, and even then

---

[12] For analysis of these developments see C.R. North, "Pentateuchal Criticism," in H. H. Rowley (ed.), *The Old Testament and Modern Study* (Oxford, 1951), 48-83; Ronald E. Clements, *One Hundred Years of Old Testament Interpretation* (Philadelphia, 1976), pp. 7-30; and Ronald E. Clements, "Pentateuchal Problems," in G.W. Anderson (ed.), *Tradition and Interpretation* (Oxford, 1979), 96-124. For the developments which preceded Wellhausen see Hans-Joachim Kraus, *Geschichte der historisch-kritischen Erforschung des Alten Testaments*, 2. Aufl. (Neukirchen-Vluyn, 1969).

[13] Gerhard von Rad, "The Form-Critical Problem of the Hexateuch," *The Problem of the Hexateuch and Other Essays*, trans. E.W. Trueman Dicken (New York, 1966), pp. 1-3.

[14] Martin Noth, *Überlieferungsgeschichtliche Studien, I* (Tübingen, 1943); *A History of Pentateuchal Traditions*, trans. Bernhard W. Anderson (Englewood Cliffs, 1972).

significant opposition must be acknowledged.[15] Yet despite these
reservations it seems safe to say that a revised documentary
hypothesis as represented in the works of von Rad and Noth
continues to be the most widely held theory. Clearly such a
consensus, in order to include the views of both von Rad and Noth,
leaves unresolved a great many details as well as the larger question
of whether the penultimate form of the Pentateuch was a Hexateuch
or a Tetrateuch. Thus with relatively minor variations Pfeiffer,
Weiser, Eissfeldt and Fohrer present an account of the formation of
the Hexateuch through a process of combining documentary
sources.[16] Each of the above then posits a politically necessitated
severing of Joshua just prior to the promulgation of the Pentateuch
by Ezra.[17]   On the other hand, Noth and Soggin assume
documentary accounts of the formation of a Tetrateuch, which was
subsequently enlarged by the addition of the book of Deuteronomy.
This comprised a Pentateuch, which was canonized ca. 400
B.C.E.[18]

We have seen that Wellhausen took the position that Ezra
brought the Hexateuch with him to Palestine, and subsequently
published the Pentateuch. As we noted, no account is given of the
circumstances or persons responsible for the final stage in the
formation of the Pentateuch, namely the separation of Joshua from
Deuteronomy. Von Rad's analysis is subject to the same critique.
He is, he informs us, at pains to reverse the atomistic trend in
hexateuchal studies, and to begin a form critical analysis of the
"genre" Hexateuch. Thus he proposes that the present canonical
"Hexateuch as we have it" be taken seriously.[19] The fact remains,

---

[15] E.g., the work of Kaufmann and Cassuto.

[16] R. H. Pfeiffer, *Introduction to the Old Testament* (New York, 1948); Artur
Weiser, *The Old Testament: Its Formation and Development*, trans. Dorothea
M. Barton (New York, 1961); Otto Eissfeldt, *The Old Testament: An
Introduction*, trans. Peter R. Ackroyd, (New York, 1965); Ernst Sellin and Georg
Fohrer, *Introduction to the Old Testament*, trans. David E. Green (Nashville and
New York, 1968).

[17] Except for Weiser, *Old Testament*, p. 138, who thinks Nehemiah published
the Pentateuch, and Pfeiffer, *Introduction*, pp. 56-58, who holds that it was
published ca. 400 B.C.E., but not by Ezra.

[18] Noth, *Pentateuchal Traditions*; J. Alberto Soggin, *Introduction to the Old
Testament*, trans. John Bowden (Philadelphia, 1976).

[19] von Rad, "Hexateuch," p. 8.

however, that in its canonical form the Torah is comprised of five, not six, books. Of this fact von Rad provides no account.

Regarding the final stage of its formation, Martin Noth's study of the Pentateuch is likewise deficient. This is because after his exhaustive investigation of the traditions of the Tetrateuch he turns to the "total Pentateuch" only to conclude that in its final form it is no longer of great traditio-historical importance. What is of significance for us, however, is his definition of the "total Pentateuch," namely: "the incorporation of the J narrative as expanded with numerous E elements into the literary framework of P."[20]   Noth is explicit, however, that J, E, and P do not extend beyond Numbers, and D is a part of the Deuteronomistic History. It remains to be explained why it is that we have a Pentateuch, and how and when the final step in its formation (the addition of Deuteronomy) was taken.

The fact that neither Wellhausen, nor von Rad, nor Noth provides a satisfactory account of the final stages in the formation of the Pentateuch is not to say that no explanation at all has been given. Since antiquity Jewish tradition has attributed the canonization of Torah to Ezra;[21]   since Wellhausen critical scholarship, with few exceptions, has done much the same.

If, as is indeed the case, scholars have long neglected the final stages in the formation of the Pentateuch, then we must ask why. Are there good reasons for this inattention?   To be sure, the resources for the history of Judah in the Persian period are exiguous at best, but Wellhausen's shift from Hexateuch to Pentateuch appears to be an oversight more amenable to a philosophical explanation. As even a casual reading of the *Prolegomena* will show, Wellhausen viewed the process of Israel's history as decline, the priestly legislation as sterile, and nascent Judaism as the culmination of all that is degenerate in institutional religion. Consistent with this interpretation of the history of Israelite religion is the last century's emphasis on the original, pristine, form of all of Israel's religious practices, institutions, and texts. It should be no surprise, then, that the final redactional stages in the formation of the Pentateuch, understood as secondary and inferior, if not spurious, alterations, and the period during which they occurred were neglected. Freed from such prejudicial assumptions, our task is to provide a more adequate account of the final stages in the formation

---

[20] Noth, *Pentateuchal Traditions*, p. 248.

[21] Cf. b. Baba Bathra 14b-15a, 2 Esdras 14:37-48.

of the Pentateuch.

Such an account, however, must await considerable research on several fronts. That some form of the documentary hypothesis is the best explanation for the composition of the Pentateuch, and that considerable further investigation of its several literary sources is now necessary, are widely shared convictions of students of the Pentateuch. Thus it is clear that the internal study of the Pentateuch (and Joshua) must be pursued with an increased interest and focus on the processes by which separate literary elements were joined in larger complexes which ultimately eventuated in the Pentateuch. On the other hand, all Jewish texts of the Second Temple period including additions to earlier works must be examined to determine their relationships to and use of pentateuchal narrative and legal traditions. Such a project would, in addition, require as full a reconstruction of the history of the Persian period as the sources will allow. Only then will it be possible to speak knowledgeably about the time, place, and processes by which Israelite tradition, both legal and narrative, was filled out, rounded off, and fixed as the Torah. My analysis of the Chronicler's use of pentateuchal legislation is intended to contribute to that larger task.

The Chronicler's History contains numerous references to an authoritative law book. In Chapter 4 I examine these references, and describe the Chronicler's assertions and apparent assumptions about the history of this torah book. I argue that he believed the book available to him was the ancient authoritative law book from Mosaic times, the same book which had ordered Israelite life throughout its history, and in accord with which the Judean Golah community had been restored. I then investigate the Chronicler's claims to the authority of this book and his descriptions of the requirements it contained in order to determine its relationship to pentateuchal legislation (Ch. 5). Since Wellhausen it has been widely affirmed that this torah book was in fact the Pentateuch. My comparative analysis, however, will raise serious questions about this identification. The Chronicler did regard laws from all of Israel's major codes (JE, D, H, P, and supplements to P) as authoritative, and combined them eclectically; but he also claimed that his torah book contained laws which are not in the Pentateuch. That leads to the conclusion that the constituent parts of the Torah canon were available to the Chronicler, but that at least as far as he was concerned the fixed Torah canon to which no changes could be made did not yet exist.

Any research on the Chronicler's History Work, however, faces serious historical and literary difficulties. Chapter 2 deals with those of an historical nature, and although limited by the paucity of available evidence attempts to describe some of the more important aspects of Judean history in the Persian period. Among these are the longstanding questions regarding the dates, nature, and context in Persian policy of the missions of Ezra and Nehemiah. I then take up the complex questions of the sources and authorship of the Chronicler's Work (Ch. 3), and conclude that like the Pentateuch it was source-based and has been expanded (most notably by the Nehemiah Memoir), but is, nevertheless, at the end of its redactional history, a literary unity.

Chapter 2

Aspects of Judean History in the Persian Period

> We are in direct need of information as to the history of
> the Jews in the Persian Period, and every scrap of
> material that provides help ought to be treasured and put
> to use. But no extremity of need can outweigh the
> obligation to follow the evidence.[1]

Unfortunately for one who would write the history of the Jews in Palestine during the Persian period, these observations, made by Torrey at the beginning of the century, remain true; our sources (inscriptional, archaeological and literary) are few and constant care must be taken not to over interpret them. The problem does not end there, however, for our sources are not only few but ambiguous. This is not to say that the situation is hopeless or that, since the sources are inadequate for a confident reconstruction of the history of the period, no such history should be attempted. What it means is that historians' goals must be modest and their conclusions tentative.

Accordingly the goal of this chapter is to sketch out a general overview of Judean history in the Persian period, which if not certain in all its details is at least true to the sources at our disposal. This historical overview is necessary in the present context for several reasons. It was during the Persian period that the temple was rebuilt and Judaism began, that (according to the standard scholarly view) the Torah canon was fixed, and the Chronicler's History Work composed. This historical overview, then, is intended to provide a reasonably reliable historical setting for our

---

[1]Charles Cutler Torrey, *Ezra Studies* (Chicago, 1910), p. 157.

subsequent investigation into the status of (what is now) pentateuchal law in the Chronicler's History.

The Return to Judah from Babylon and the
Rebuilding of the Temple

For the Jews the Persian period began when Cyrus, to the delight of the priests of Marduk, wrested Babylon from the absent and (from these priests' point of view) apostate Nabonidus. This turn of events, not completely unanticipated or unwelcomed in Babylonian Jewish circles,[2] was of major significance for the subsequent history and religion of the Jews because one of Cyrus' first actions after taking Babylon was to authorize and support a return to Judah and the restoration of the temple.[3] Cyrus' behavior should not be thought to reflect some special sympathy for the exiled Jews, but was a part of a general policy of politically expedient religious toleration from which the Jews among others benefited. The results of this policy are described by the Cyrus Cylinder as follows:

> As to the region from...as far as Ashur and Susa, Agade, Eshnunna, the towns Zamban, Me-Turnu, Der as well as the region of the Gutians, I returned to these sacred cities on the other side of the Tigris, the sanctuaries of which have been ruins for a long time, the images which used to live therein and established for them permanent sanctuaries. I also gathered all their former inhabitants and returned to them their habitations. Furthermore, I resettled upon the command of Marduk, the great lord, all the gods of Sumer and Akkad whom Nabonidus has brought into Babylon to the anger of the lord of the gods, unharmed, in their former chapels, the places which make them happy.[4]

---

[2]See e.g., Second Isaiah (Is. 44:28-45:13).

[3]Ezra 1:2-4; cf. 6:3-5.

[4]The translation is from James B. Pritchard (ed.), *Ancient Near Eastern Texts Relating to the Old Testament* (Princeton, 1950), p. 316.

Unquestionably this is a propagandistic account,[5] and it refers to cultic centers on the other side of the Tigris and not in what would become the satrapy "Beyond the River" (i.e., the Euphrates) of which Judah was a part. Nevertheless the basic claim is widely regarded as historical, and thus provides a very likely context in Persian policy for the edict of Cyrus in Ezra 1:2-4 (cf. 6:3-5)[6] by which he authorized a return to Jerusalem and the rebuilding of the temple at the expense of the royal treasury. In addition, the tradition claims that Cyrus returned the sacred vessels plundered by Nebuchadrezzar. These were delivered to the prince of Judah (נשיא), one Sheshbazzar, who was appointed "governor" (פחה)[7] by Cyrus and entrusted with the return of the vessels and the rebuilding of the temple (Ezra 1:7-11, 5:14-15). This latter he apparently started, but it fell to his successors in the reign of Darius I, the Davidid Zerubbabel and Jeshua the priest (high priest according to Haggai and Zechariah), to complete it. Sheshbazzar remains a mysterious figure, however, for nothing further is said of him.[8] The Chronicler, whether out of ignorance or by design, seems to confuse Sheshbazzar with Zerubbabel, whose activity was clearly later during the reign of Darius.[9]

---

[5] A.T. Olmstead, *History of the Persian Empire* (Chicago, 1948), pp. 51-52.

[6] The fact that 6:3-5 is in Aramaic need not be taken as evidence that it is more original than the Hebrew version of the decree in 1:2-4. Cf. Peter R. Ackroyd, *Israel Under Babylon and Persia*, The New Clarendon Bible, Old Testament, IV (Oxford, 1970), pp. 202-203.

[7] Usually translated "governor", the term can have a range of meanings. Here it probably refers to a commissioner with a limited appointment. Cf. Peter R. Ackroyd, "Israel in the Exilic and Post-Exilic Periods," in G.W. Anderson (ed.) *Tradition and Interpretation* (Oxford, 1979), p. 338; and *Israel Under Babylon and Persia*, p. 204.

[8] Albright identified him with the Davidid Shenazzar who is mentioned in 1 Chron. 3:18. See W.F. Albright, *The Biblical Period from Abraham to Ezra*, revised and expanded ed. (New York, 1963), p. 86. This view is taken up in J.A. Bright, *A History of Israel*, 2nd ed. (London, 1972), p. 362. Cf. Geo Widengren, "The Persian Period," in John H. Hayes and J. Maxwell Miller (eds.) *Israelite and Judean History*, the Old Testament Library (Philadelphia, 1977) p. 520, who disputes this identification.

[9] Cf. Haggai's chronology, R.A. Bowman, *Introduction and Exegesis to the Book of Ezra and the Book of Nehemiah*, The Interpreter's Bible, III (New York and Nashville, 1954), p. 574.

The empire of Cyrus, at his death in 530 B.C.E., passed in an orderly way to his son Cambyses. Succession would not always be orderly or peaceful; that it was in this instance is due to the fact that Cyrus very early on identified Cambyses as his heir, and subsequently allowed him the title "King of Babylon."[10] Spared the trouble of defending the legitimacy of his rule at home, Cambyses immediately set out to expand the empire in the West. He launched a campaign against Egypt and brought it under Persian rule in 525 B.C.E. According to Herodotus Cambyses was insane and his rule of Egypt was despotic from start to finish. It is said that he desecrated the corpse of Amasis, killed an Apis bull, persecuted priests and defiled temples.[11]   At a later date (407 B.C.E.) the Jews at Elephantine in the context of a request for authorization to rebuild their temple observed that Cambyses had destroyed all the temples of Egypt, but had spared theirs.[12]   If all this were true one would have to conclude that Cyrus' policy of religious toleration did not survive his death.

There are reasons to be skeptical of this description, however. Olmstead refutes "the oft-repeated slander" that Cambyses killed an Apis bull and cites several pictoral and inscriptional representations of him acknowledging Egyptian dieties; one of his appointees, the governor of Coptos, is even said to have assisted in getting stones for the rebuilding of temples.[13]   The important inscription of Udjahorresnet, a priest of the goddess Neith at the temple in Sais, written in the reign of Darius, claims that Cambyses went to Sais, acknowledged the religion of Egypt, took an Egyptian throne name (Re-mesuti, born of Re), purified the temple and restored the ancient festivals.[14]

Gray, who describes this conflicting evidence, believes that the accounts of Cambyses' violent and sacrilegious governance of Egypt, while exaggerated, are not without some basis in historical fact. His conclusion is that Cambyses' initial toleration was abandoned after his failed attempt to conquer Ethiopia either

---

[10]Olmstead, *History*, pp. 86-87.

[11]Heroditus, III, 16, 29, 37.

[12]*AP*, 30. Cf. A.E. Cowley, *Aramaic Papyri of the Fifth Century BC* (London, 1923), pp. 108-19.

[13]Olmstead, *History*, pp. 89-90.

[14]Martin Noth, *The History of Israel*, 2nd ed., trans. Peter R. Ackroyd (London, 1960), p. 305; Olmstead, *History*, p. 91.

because, as Herodotus claimed, he went mad, or perhaps in retaliation for priestly involvement in conspiracies against him in his absence.[15] While it must be readily admitted that the evidence does not allow any certainty about this, his suggestion is quite possible. The Udjahorresnet inscription, Gray suggests, includes a vague reference to this change in policy when it speaks of "the heavy misfortune which had befalled the whole land."[16]   And the correspondence from Elephantine, referred to above, includes a text which associates the Egyptian destruction of the temple of Yahu in 410 B.C.E. with Egyptian rebellion against Persia and claims that "we (the Jews) did not leave our posts, and nothing disloyal was found in us."[17]   Thus it is stressed that the Jews were loyal and the Egyptians not. In this context it seems possible that the preservation or destruction of temples by Cambyses was not a matter of whim or insanity, but rather a more properly political than religious policy which encouraged and recognized loyalty. As Ackroyd has noted, "there was not a little of political skill in the policy."[18]

We have no specific information about events and conditions in Judah during the reign of Cambyses. But from the brief descriptions of conditions just prior to 520 B.C.E. in Haggai 1:1-11, we may surmise that the initiative of Sheshbazzar had been abandoned in the face of famine and drought. In difficult times the people of Judah sought to secure their own dwellings and left the temple in ruins, their view apparently being that rebuilding the temple would have to await better times. The prophet, of course, explains the hard times as the direct consequence of the people's failure to rebuild the house of Yahweh (1:9-11).

While Cambyses was still occupied in the West his brother Bardiya usurped the Persian throne.[19]   Cambyses began the

---

[15]G. Buchanan Gray, "The Foundation and Extension of the Persian Empire," in J.B. Bury, S.A. Cook and F.E. Adcock (eds.) *The Cambridge Ancient History, IV, The Persian Empire and the West* (New York, 1926), pp. 22-23.

[16]Gray, "Persian Empire," p. 23.

[17]*AP*, 27 lines 1-2.

[18]Ackroyd, *Israel Under Babylon and Persia*, p. 165.

[19]According to the Behistun inscription Bardiya was an imposter, one Gaumata, the real Bardiya having been secretly murdered by Cambyses before he attacked Egypt. Widengren, "The Persian Period," p. 521, accepts the claims of the inscription as historically accurate, but see Ackroyd, *Israel Under Babylon and*

journey back to Babylon to deal with the insurrection, but died by his own hand enroute.[20]   It was Darius who finally after a year of fighting killed Bardiya in 522 B.C.E.

The captive peoples, including the Jews of Judah, were not unaware of the political turmoil in Babylon at this time. This chaos, especially the murder of Bardiya, "brought renewed hopes of national independence which bred a perfect orgy of revolts among the subject peoples."[21]   In Judah this resulted, it would appear from Haggai and Zechariah 1-8, in the renewed nationalism and messianism which precipitated the reconstruction of the temple under Zerubbabel and the identification of the latter as messiah.

A somewhat different and more detailed account of this period is provided by Ezra 3-6. The chronology of events and the literary history of these chapters remain vexing problems which cannot be altogether resolved here. Clearly, the Chronicler in chapter 3 has confused Sheshbazzar with Zerubbabel and Cyrus with Darius.[22] It is also generally agreed that the correspondence between the opponents of the Jews and Artaxerxes regarding the rebuilding of Jerusalem's walls (neither letter mentions the temple) is out of place in its present context and belongs to the period of Nehemiah almost a century later.[23]   Finally, after a long period of skepticism, the Aramaic texts which purport to be authentic documents are widely held to be genuine, although edited, copies of exactly what they claim to be.[24]

The date in Ezra 3:8 is not clear since the reference point, when they came to the temple (site), is not known. A comparison with Haggai and Zechariah raises the possibility that this originally referred to the second year of Darius. In any case, the dating is so clear in Haggai that one may take the present text as describing the events commencing in 520 B.C.E. (i.e., Darius' second year)

Persia, pp. 165-67, who points out their propagandistic nature. So also Olmstead, *History*, pp. 108-109.

[20]Olmstead, *History*, p. 108. Herodotus, III, 62-66 describes it as an accident.

[21]Olmstead, *History*, p. 110.

[22]Cf. e.g., Bowman, *Ezra and Nehemiah*, p. 589.

[23]Jacob M. Myers, *Ezra. Nehemiah. Introduction, Translation, and Notes*, The Anchor Bible, XIV (Garden City, 1965), p. 34, reviews the literature.

[24]That is, the letter to Artaxerxes (Ezra 4:11-16), his response (4:17-22), the letter to Darius (5:7-17), and Darius' reply (6:6-12), as well as Cyrus's decree (6:3-5), and Ezra's commission (7:12-26). Bowman, *Ezra and Nehemiah*, pp. 557-58, and Widengren, "The Persian Period," pp. 495-99, review the literature.

without deciding whether it has been damaged in transmission or was originally unclear. The text describes a rebuilding of the altar and the restoration of the sacrificial cult beginning with the feast of booths. No one supposes that the description of the liturgy is an accurate account of what transpired at the beginning of the restoration prior even to the rebuilding of the temple; the text is usually taken, and valued, as a description of the cultus as the Chronicler knew it or wished it to be. The rebuilding of the altar, on the other hand, is something that one would expect to have been accomplished long before Zerubbabel, especially if the reconstruction of the temple was initiated by Sheshbazzar. Rudolph assigns the event to the second or third year of Cyrus, thus crediting Sheshbazzar, not Zerubbabel and Jeshua, with rebuilding the altar.[25]

If that is true, then with verse 8 we have come forward almost twenty years to the period of Darius, during which, under the leadership of Zerubbabel and Jeshua and with the encouragement of the prophets Haggai and Zechariah, the temple was rebuilt. The present text, however, makes no mention of the prophets' role. It stresses instead, and this is absent in Haggai and Zechariah, the roles of the priests and Levites and that the work was undertaken by returned exiles. This latter theme is continued in chapter 4 which narrates how the people of the land, who claimed to worship Yahweh, wanted to help the returnees with the work of rebuilding but were refused on the grounds that the task had been commissioned to exiles by Cyrus (v. 3). This group then sought to frustrate the reconstruction and did so successfully until 520 B.C.E. (v. 24). As we have seen, the Chronicler has merged the period of Sheshbazzar with its unsuccessful building program with the later period of Zerubbabel and the completion of the work Sheshbazzar had started. His view is that early in the reign of Cyrus Zerubbabel (it was actually Sheshbazzar) started to rebuild but was impeded until the second year of Darius.

At this point, perhaps following another source, the Chronicler describes the events of 520-515 B.C.E. (Ezra 5:1-6:18). In this version Haggai and Zechariah play an important, but secondary, role and the local officials act responsibly not malevolently. Tattenai, the governor of Beyond the River, inquired of the Jews who had authorized the rebuilding in which they were engaged, but did not

---

[25]Wilhelm Rudolph, *Esra und Nehemia mit 3. Esra*, Handbuch zum Alten Testament, 20/1 (Tübingen, 1949), p. 29.

force them to abandon the project pending the discovery of Darius' wishes in the matter (5:3-5). The Chronicler at this point in the story introduces Tattenai's letter (5:7-17) which then carries the narrative. According to this letter, the reconstruction of the temple was progressing well, and the Jews, when questioned, claimed that Cyrus had decreed that the temple be rebuilt and had given the project to Sheshbazzar, who had begun the work that was yet to be completed. Tattenai concludes his letter with the polite suggestion that Darius investigate whether in fact Cyrus had made such a decree. This Darius did. A search was made, and the document was found (6:1-5). In his reply to Tattenai, Darius reaffirms Cyrus' edict and himself decrees that the costs of rebuilding be provided to the Jews out of the royal revenue from Beyond the River together with sacrifices to be made on behalf of the king and his sons (6:6-11). Darius concludes with a curse on anyone who would oppose his will by altering the edict or damaging the temple.

The king's support of a project which his most highly placed local representative, Tattenai, regarded as at least potentially threatening is initially surprising.[26] His rule is not yet stable at home, how can he allow a province to nurture independence?

Some light is shed on this question by the Gadatas inscription,[27] according to which Darius reprimanded Gadatas, his administrator in western Asian Minor as follows:

> The king of kings, Darius, son of Hystaspes, to his slave Gadatas, thus speaks: I have learned that you do not in all respects obey my injunctions...because you set at naught *my policy towards the gods*, I will give you, if you do not change, a proof of my injured feelings. For your have enforced tribute from the holy gardeners of Apollo and have ordered them to dig unhallowed

---

[26]Olmstead, *History*, p. 140, notes that Tattenai had "taken down in writing the names of the elders who were conducting the work, ready to punish them if their extraordinary claim [to have the permission of Cyrus] proved to be false." Cf. Ezra 5:4, 10.

[27] Although the inscription is in Greek and comes from Roman times and is therefore not an autograph, it is based on an authentic original. See A.T. Olmstead, *History of Palestine and Syria to the Macedonian Conquest* (New York and London, 1931), pp. 571-72; Ackroyd, *Israel Under Babylon and Persia*, p. 199; and Noth, *History*, p. 305.

ground, *not knowing the mind of my forefathers toward the god...*(emphasis added).[28]

This inscription is important for two reasons. It states what we infer from other texts at our disposal: there was a general Persian policy with regard to the religion of captive peoples, a part of which is clearly the support of established (traditional) official prerogatives. Secondly, like the correspondence in Ezra 5-6, it presents Darius as one who took seriously and identified himself with the decisions of his predecessors. Why exactly he did so we can only guess. It seems likely that in the case of the Jerusalem temple it was precisely because of the instability at the beginning of his reign that "he found it expedient to confirm Cyrus' edict and thereby to gain the good will of the Jews who could form for him a buffer against Egypt."[29] Whatever Darius' motives, his decree was effective. The Chronicler's Aramaic source concludes with the statement that Tattenai and his associates complied with Darius' wishes and that through the prophesying of Haggai and Zechariah, the command of God, and the decree of Cyrus and Darius, the temple was finished and dedicated in the sixth year of Darius' reign (6:13-18).[30]

With the completion of the temple the little light that our sources shed on Judean history in the sixth century is extinguished. Not until the periods of Ezra and Nehemiah will we have evidence for an historical reconstruction and even then intractable problems of chronology will remain. For the first half of the fifth century we have only Malachi, whose no doubt one-sided portrayal suggests a Judean community not much interested in strict religious practice.[31] Priests despise Yahweh by offering impure sacrifices (1:6-8) and false torah (2:7-9). The people have profaned the covenant and sanctuary by marrying foreigners (2:11-12), they have robbed God

---

[28] Quoted in Olmstead, *Palestine and Syria*, p. 571.

[29] Bowman, *Ezra and Nehemiah*, p. 616.

[30] "Artaxerxes" in Ezra 6:14 is a later addition. See Myers, *Ezra. Nehemiah*, p. 53; and Peter R. Ackroyd, *1 and 2 Chronicles, Ezra, Nehemiah: Introduction and Commentary*, Torch Bible Commentaries (London, 1973), p. 237.

[31] It is very difficult to date Malachi. The temple is in use so it is later than Haggai and Zechariah 1-8. Cf. Ackroyd, "Israel in the Exilic and Post-Exilic Periods," p. 332, and *Israel Under Babylon and Persia*, p. 243. But it is prior to Nehemiah. See Jacob M. Myers, *The World of the Restoration* (Englewood Cliffs, 1968), pp. 96-103.

by not tithing (3:8-10), and there are among them sorcerers, adulterers, those who swear falsely and those who oppress the community's lower stratum (3:5). For all this, declares the prophet, judgment must come (3:1-3, 19-21) after which a refined priesthood and "those who feared the Lord" (3:16) will enjoy Yahweh's blessing (3:3-4, 17, 20-21).

The Order of Ezra and Nehemiah

The next episode of Judean history for which we have any evidence is either the period of Ezra's mission or that of Nehemiah depending on which came first. But deciding that question has been, and I believe will remain, one of the most difficult problems of Hebrew Bible criticism in spite of considerable effort.[32]

The traditional chronology, based on the narrative sequence of the present arrangement of Ezra-Nehemiah, is as follows:

1) Ezra arrived in Jerusalem on the first day of the fifth month of the seventh year of Artaxerxes (Ezra 7:7-9).
2) In the ninth month (no year given, but by implication the seventh year) Ezra dealt with the problem of mixed marriages (Ezra 9-10).
3) Thirteen years later, in the first month of the twentieth year of Artaxerxes, Nehemiah risked a less than cheerful audience with the king and won an appointment as governor (פחה) of Judah with a commission to rebuild Jerusalem (Neh. 2:1-8; 5:14).
4) Within six months of this commission, despite internal problems of economic oppression and external opposition, the wall of Jerusalem was finished (Neh. 2:9-6:15).
5) In the seventh month (no year specified, but by implication still the twentieth year of Artaxerxes) Ezra read from the law of Moses in the presence of Nehemiah (Neh. 8:1-9).

---

[32] The literature is reviewed at length in H.H., Rowley, "The Chronological Order of Ezra and Nehemiah," *Ignace Goldziher Memorial Volume* 1, eds., S. Löwinger and J. Somogyi (Budapest, 1948), pp. 117-49 = H.H. Rowley, *The Servant of the Lord*, 2nd ed. (Oxford, 1965), pp. 137-68; and Ulrich Kellermann, "Erwägungen zum Problem der Esradatierung," *ZAW*, LXXX (1968), 55-87.

6) Nehemiah remained in Judah until the thirty-second year of Artaxerxes (Neh. 5:14); he returned to Babylon for an unspecified period and then came again to Jerusalem (Neh. 13:6-7).

In sum, Ezra's mission preceded that of Nehemiah although to some extent the two overlapped. That the Artaxerxes in whose twentieth year Nehemiah came to Jerusalem was the first of that name (Artaxerxes I, Longimanus, 465-424 B.C.E.) is now widely regarded as a fixed datum[33] from which it follows that Ezra, who came prior in this monarch's seventh year, must have arrived in 458 B.C.E.

Several questions arise from this traditional chronology. In the first place, it seems strange that Ezra and Nehemiah, whose missions according to the theory overlapped, would be mentioned together so infrequently.[34] It is the case, moreover, that the few texts which do associate the two men as contemporaries are all suspect.[35] Rowley is surely right that "(W)herever their names are found together one is a mere passenger, whose name can be dropped without the slightest consequence to the narrative."[36]

Secondly, the thirteen-year delay between Ezra's arrival in Jerusalem and his reading of the law, which was after all the purpose of his mission, is inexplicable. He is sent to make inquiries about Judean observance of the law (Ezra 7:14), and is charged with appointing officials to teach and enforce it (Ezra 7:25-26). In addition to this, Ezra is to transport a considerable treasure (7:15-17). We are told in explicit detail of Ezra's discharge of the later obligation: four days after his arrival the treasure was turned over to Meremoth, Eleazar, Jozabad and Noadiah. Are we to believe he waited thirteen years to read the law? With what justification could he in 458 deal with the problem of inter-marriage, a violation of "thy commandments" (Ezra 9:10, 14), "according to the law" (10:3) if he

---

[33] It is, nevertheless, possible that Nehemiah should be dated during the reign of Artaxerxes II. See Richard J. Saley, "The Date of Nehemiah Reconsidered," *Biblical and Near Eastern Studies, Essays in Honor of William Sanford LaSor*, ed. Gary A. Tuttle (Grand Rapids, 1978), pp. 151-65.

[34] They are explicitly associated with each other only at Neh. 8:9 and 12:26, and implicitly by the context at Neh. 10:2 (Ev. 10:1), and 12:36.

[35] Frank Moore Cross, "A Reconstruction of the Judean Restoration," *JBL*, XCIV (1975), p. 8.

[36] H.H. Rowley, "Chronological Order," p. 165.

did not read and expound the law until 445? The answer, of course, is that he did not. The narrative of Ezra's reading of the law (Neh. 8-9) is out of sequence in the period of Nehemiah and in fact the mission of Ezra did not overlap that of Nehemiah.[37]

If their missions do not overlap, then according to the traditional view we must assume that Ezra came and left before Nehemiah arrived in Jerusalem. But we have just seen that the narrative sequence of Ezra-Nehemiah, on which this view depends, is unreliable. And moreover, the Chronicler's confusion regarding the chronology and identity of Zerubbabel and Sheshbazzar as well as Cyrus and Darius (Ezra 3) can only increase the skepticism with which one regards his view of the chronology of Ezra and Nehemiah.

As I have noted above, the literature on the problem of the relative chronology of Ezra and Nehemiah is immense. No attempt to review it in detail will be made here. For our purposes it must suffice to point out the major scholarly positions, of which there are three, and to provide a brief account of the basis on which I have with the greatest caution assigned the mission of Ezra to the seventh year of Artaxerxes II, Mnemon (i.e., 398 B.C.E.). A number of positions on this issue have been argued. Torrey denied that Ezra existed and thus resolved the problem of his dates,[38] while Jellicoe suspected the Chronicler of consciously switching the dates of Ezra and Nehemiah both of whom came in the reign of the first Artaxerxes.[39] These have not attracted large followings.

For most scholars the basic question on which the date of Ezra's mission turns is which Artaxerxes, Artaxerxes I, Longimanus (465-424) or Artaxerxes II, Mnemon (404-358), is meant in Ezra 7:7-8 which states that Ezra's arrival in Jerusalem was in the seventh year of Artaxerxes the king. This decision gives us the two most widely held positions: the traditional view still championed by many that Ezra came in the seventh year of Artaxerxes I, Longimanus (i.e., 458 B.C.E.) and the view proposed

[37] Widengren, "The Persian Period," pp. 504-505. A few scholars argue that the missions of Ezra and Nehemiah did in fact overlap. See Rudolph, *Esra und Nehemia*, p. 71; and Bright, *History*, pp. 392-403.
[38] Torrey, *Ezra Studies*, pp. 238-48. Cf. Loring W. Batten, *A Critical and Exegetical Commentary on the Books of Ezra and Nehemiah*, The International Critical Commentary (Edinburgh, 1913), p. 51, for a refutation of this claim.
[39] Sidney Jellicoe, "Nehemiah--Ezra: A Reconstruction," *Expository Times*, LIX (1947-48), p. 54.

and vigorously advanced by van Hoonacker that Ezra arrived in the seventh year of Artaxerxes II, Mnemon (i.e., 398 B.C.E.).[40]

The third major option is proposed by a relatively small number of scholars who conjecturally emend the text of Ezra 7:7-8 from the "seventh" to the "twenty-seventh"[41] or "thirty-seventh"[42] year of Artaxerxes (Longimanus) resulting in dates of 438 or 428 B.C.E. Since the text itself provides no warrant for either emendation,[43] and since, moreover, the supposed loss of "twenty" or "thirty" would have to have occurred not once but twice (Ezra 7:7 and 8), this position is the least likely of the major options.[44] This leaves us with a date for Ezra of either 458 or 398 B.C.E.

At either date it would have been politically astute of the Persians to give such authority and support to Ezra. In 460 B.C.E. the Egyptian Inarus, with the help of the Athenians, led a nationalistic revolt against Persia which was not quashed until 454.[45] At about the same time, ca. 450 B.C.E., Megabyzus, the Persian satrap of Beyond the River, launched a short-lived revolt.[46] Clearly in the middle of the fifth century the western reaches of the Persian empire were in turmoil and threatened the integrity and stability of the empire as a whole. Some have found in these events the historical context of the missions of Ezra and Nehemiah respectively.[47] The Jews of Palestine had historically played the superpowers off of each other and could be expected to glimpse their own independence in the revolt of Egypt. Shrewdly, the Persians insured the loyalty of the Judean Jews by sending Ezra in 458 B.C.E. The mission of Nehemiah was later (445 B.C.E.) and

---

[40] A. van Hoonacker, "Néhémie et Esdras, une nouvelle hypothèse sur la chronologie de l'époque de la restauration, "*Le Museon*, IX (1890), pp. 151-84, 317-51, 389-401, and a series of publications cited with the above in Rowley, "Chronological Order," p. 138 n. 4.

[41] Bowman, *Ezra and Nehemiah*, p. 563, attributes this innovation to Wellhausen.

[42] Rudolph, *Esra und Nehemia*, pp. 65-71; Bright, *History*, pp. 392-403.

[43] Bowman, *Ezra and Nehemiah*, p. 624.

[44] Ackroyd, "Israel in the Exilic and Post-Exilic Periods," pp. 333-34. J.A. Emerton, "Did Ezra Go to Jerusalem in 438 B.C.?," *JTS*, XVII (1966), 1-19, is a convincing refutation of Bright's affirmative.

[45] Ackroyd, "Israel in the Exilic and Post-Exilic Periods," p. 334.

[46] Olmstead, *History*, p. 312.

[47] E.g., Olmstead, *History*, pp. 303-308, 312-17.

was intended to stabilize Judah in the wake of the aborted revolt of Megabyzus (ca. 450). Others, who date Ezra's mission in 398 B.C.E., view the revolts of Inarus and Megabyzus as the context for the mission of Nehemiah.[48] The historical context of Ezra's mission would then be the similar but more ominous, from the Persian perspective, events of the turn of the century. In the Elephantine papyri we find Jewish accusations of Egyptian disloyalty to Persia coming from the years 410-407 B.C.E.[49] Within a few years Egypt was in full revolt and by 399 Nepherites I had founded the independent twenty-ninth dynasty.[50] The Jewish outpost at Yeb most likely suffered at this time a fate that "can scarcely have been happy,"[51] and Egyptian control may have been extended on into Palestine.[52] Ezra's mission in 398 is then construed as a Persian attempt to stabilize Beyond the River and more specifically to prevent Judah from falling into an Egyptian orbit.[53]

If it be admitted that conditions in the West were such as to warrant the commission of Ezra in either 458 or 398 B.C.E., it follows that a determination of which is the correct date must be based on an analysis of the relevant extant literary evidence, which, regrettably, is limited to texts in Ezra and Nehemiah.

It is generally agreed among those who have addressed this issue that the evidence on which we depend is inadequate to the task of conclusively dating Ezra's mission. I opt for 398 B.C.E., therefore, with appropriate and legitimate reserve

The major reasons for this decision will follow; individually they are inconclusive, taken together they weigh in favor of 398 but fall short of proof.

1) Nehemiah in his memoirs takes no notice of Ezra, while the Ezra story ignores Nehemiah. If Ezra arrived in Jerusalem in 458 B.C.E. and established the law in the following years, then it is remarkable that Nehemiah

---

[48] Noth, *History*, pp. 318-19; Ackroyd, *Israel Under Babylon and Persia*, p. 175; Widengren, "The Persian Period," p. 529.

[49] *AP* 27.

[50] Olmstead, *History*, p. 383.

[51] Olmstead, *History*, p. 374.

[52] Olmstead, *History*, p. 383.

[53] H. Cazelles, "La mission d'Esdras," *VT*, IV (1954), 132; Widengren, "The Persian Period," p. 535.

arriving thirteen years later would fail to refer to him or to the fact that it was his law that he found in effect. On the other hand, if Ezra came some fifty years after Nehemiah, we need not be surprised that Nehemiah is unmentioned in the Ezra narrative.[54]

2) Nehemiah reviews the list of those who returned to Judah with Zerubbabel (Neh. 7:5-7), but makes no reference to the estimated five thousand persons who came with Ezra.[55] This group is again ignored when Nehemiah refers to the Judean Jews not as the "sons of the exile" but as those who "escaped exile" (Neh. 1:2-3).

3) Nehemiah appears to have arrived in a virtually uninhabited Jerusalem and took steps to increase its population (Neh. 7:4; 11:1-2), while in the period of Ezra Jerusalem seems to be well established (Ezra 10:1).[56]

4) Both Ezra and Nehemiah found it necessary to deal with the problem of mixed marriages. In light of the fact that Malachi, too, speaks to this subject (Mal. 2:10-16) it seems safe to assume that such marriages were a not-infrequent practice throughout the Persian period. It is possible that Ezra's attempts to deal with the problem in 458 were unsuccessful and that Nehemiah was a few years later faced with the same issue. A more likely scenario, however, is that Nehemiah's *ad hoc* treatment of a longstanding problem was precipitated by the personal affront of the marriage of the high priest's grandson to the daughter of Sanballat, Nehemiah's archenemy (Neh. 13:23-28). This marriage apparently took place between Nehemiah's administrations while he was in Babylon. On his return Nehemiah dealt with the problem of intermarriage in general, and this marriage in particular, with spontaneous violence (Neh. 13:25, 28). And while he cites the ancient precedent of Solomon (v. 26) and virtually quotes Deuteronomy (Neh. 13:25; Deut. 7:3), he makes no mention of Ezra's efforts to deal with the problem which had resulted in a solution to which, if Ezra came in 458 B.C.E., many in Nehemiah's Jerusalem

---

[54] Rowley, "Chronological Order," pp. 160-61.

[55] Widengren, "The Persian Period," p. 505.

[56] Rowley, "Chronological Order," p. 152.

must have already assented (cf. Ezra 9-10). Why not remind them? It is more likely that some thirty years after Nehemiah's personal interventions Ezra appeared in 398 B.C.E. with the authority to enforce torah and that he dealt with foreign marriages according to torah and in such a way as to secure the willing consent of the populace.[57]

5) During his second administration Nehemiah appointed four persons as treasurers over the storehouses (Neh. 13:13). When Ezra arrived in Jerusalem he found a similar group of four to which he transferred the silver, gold, and vessels which he had brought from Babylon (Ezra 8:33-34).[58]

6) One of the four, perhaps their chief, to whom Ezra turned over the treasures just mentioned is one Meremoth ben Uriah (Ezra 8:33), who is also credited with repairing not one but two sections of the city wall in the period of Nehemiah (Neh. 3:4, 21). If Ezra preceded Nehemiah, we must assume either a very young Meremoth in a position of great responsibility in 458 who was still young enough thirteen years later to rebuild two sections of the wall or a mature treasurer in 458 who enjoyed an extraordinarily vigorous old age. "On the other hand, if he were a youthful enthusiast of twenty in 444 B.C., in 397 B.C., when Ezra found him already at the head of the treasury of the Temple, he would be sixty-seven. In this there is no improbability whatever."[59]

7) Nehemiah was a contemporary of the high priest Eliashib (Neh. 3:1, 20-21; 13:4, 7, 28), while Ezra was a contemporary of the former's grandson Jehohanan (Ezra 10:6; Neh. 12:10-11, 22),[60] who was, according to a papyrus from Elephantine, high priest in 410 B.C.E.[61]

---

[57] Bowman, *Ezra and Nehemiah*, p. 563.

[58] Rowley, "Chronological Order," p. 162.

[59] Rowley, "Chronological Order," p. 167.

[60] Rowley, "Chronological Order," p. 153; Widengren, "The Persian Period," p. 505.

[61] *AP* 30. See Cowley, *Papyri*, pp. 108-19.

The Mission of Nehemiah

Having opted on the basis of the literary evidence in Ezra and Nehemiah for the view that Ezra followed Nehemiah to Jerusalem in 398 B.C.E., we turn now to the mission of Nehemiah, who received his commission from Artaxerxes I in 445 B.C.E. (Neh. 2:1). Our primary evidence for this period is the so-called Nehemiah Memoir which may or may not have been originally composed by Nehemiah, but is in any case a distinctly one-sided presentation.[62] It comes to us in the book of Nehemiah with long sections of interpolated Ezra material as well as several lists, although the memoir itself seems not to have been much modified.[63]

We are informed by this source that Nehemiah, a cup bearer of Artaxerxes, received in Susa some visitors from Judah (Neh. 1:1-2).[64] The event is dated in Chislev of the king's twentieth regnal year (Neh. 1:1), but in light of Neh. 2:1, which dates a subsequent event in Nisan of the same year, it is best with Rudolph to date the visit in the nineteenth year of Artaxerxes.[65] In any event, Nehemiah inquired of his guests as to the circumstances of Judean Jewry and the city Jerusalem. It is not impossible, although the text does not mention it, that Nehemiah's visitors were in fact a

---

[62] The Nehemiah Memoir is comprised of Neh. 1:1-7:5a; 11:1-2; 12:27-43; 13:4-14 (ignoring minor glosses). See Ulrich Kellermann, *Nehemia: Quellen, Überlieferung und Geschichte*, BZAW, CII (Berlin, 1967), pp. 8-56. Kellermann identifies three strata in the book of Nehemiah, a document written by Nehemiah belonging to the genre "*Gebet der Angeklagten*" (pp. 84-86), a redaction by the Chronicler, and a post-Chronicler redaction (see the chart on his pp. 55-56). Others, who share the view that the Nehemiah source was authored by Nehemiah, would assign it to a different genre (Memorial Inscription, etc.). Kellermann reviews these hypotheses (pp. 76-84). Ackroyd, *Israel Under Babylon and Persia*, pp. 179, 247-49, doubts that Nehemiah wrote it. See Bowman, *Ezra and Nehemiah*, p. 555 for a survey of scholarly opinions on the exact original limits of the memoir.

[63] Rudolph, *Esra und Nehemia*, pp. 211-12.

[64] The apparent leader of the group, Hanani, was the brother of Nehemiah (cf. Neh. 7:2). Myers, *Ezra. Nehemiah*, p. 93; Ackroyd, *1 and 2 Chronicles, Ezra, Nehemiah*, p. 265.

[65] Rudolph, *Esra und Nehemia*, p. 102. Myers, *Ezra. Nehemiah*, p. 92, suggests that perhaps Artaxerxes' twentieth year was thought to have begun in the autumn, in which case the event of Chislev, the third month, could be followed by that of Nisan, the seventh month, both in the twentieth year.

delegation sent to the king by the leaders in Jerusalem over the heads of the bureaucratic intermediaries in Samaria to describe the situation in Judah in hope of securing permission to rebuild the walls of Jerusalem.[66]   If so they found a valuable ally in Nehemiah, who was greatly distressed to learn that the walls of Jerusalem were breached and the gates to the city burned.

It is not clear whether their report referred to the events of 587 B.C.E. or to something more recent, however Ezra 4:7-23, which is out of chronological sequence in its present context, may be relevant. The text incorporates correspondence between Rehum, the governor in Samaria, and Artaxerxes (presumably I),[67] in which Rehum informed the king that the Jews were rebuilding Jerusalem's walls. He pointed out that the city had a deserved reputation as a hotbed of rebellion, and claimed that if the rebuilding project were allowed to be completed it would be at great cost to the king. Artaxerxes replied that the work was to be stopped, and his decree was immediately and forcibly effected (Ezra 4:23).   Olmstead provides a plausible historical setting for this correspondence in the middle of the fifth century.[68]   Encouraged by the revolt of Megabyzus ca. 450 B.C.E., the Jews were, as Rehum claimed, rebuilding the walls and preparing to rebel. They did not succeed and their work was destroyed.   Perhaps it was this recent destruction, then, which was reported to Nehemiah.[69]

Nehemiah responded to the news by weeping, mourning, fasting, and praying. But when the opportunity occurred, he spoke to the king. The tone of the conversation as it is recorded in Neh. 2:2-8 suggests both that Nehemiah was well regarded by the king and that it was at some risk to himself that he spoke out about his personal concerns for Jerusalem. The conversation, nevertheless, was a complete success. Nehemiah came away with a royal appointment (apparently of twelve years duration, cf. Neh. 2:6;

---

[66] Olmstead, *History*, p. 314.

[67] Olmstead, *History*, p. 313; Ackroyd, *1 and 2 Chronicles, Ezra, Nehemiah*, p. 230.

[68] Olmstead, *History*, p. 313.

[69] Nehemiah's response to the description of the walls is hardly appropriate if his visitors referred to the destruction of 587 B.C.E., nearly a century-and-a-half prior. Ackroyd, *1 and 2 Chronicles, Ezra, Nehemiah*, p. 266.

5:14) to rebuild the city.[70]   He also received from the king letters to the governors in Beyond the River (2:7) and a military escort (2:9) to secure safe passage, as well as a letter authorizing him to use timber from the royal forest in his construction.

Shortly after his arrival, Nehemiah and a few chosen men went on a secret night-time tour of inspection to assess exactly the condition of the walls and gates of Jerusalem. He then announced to the populace that he had a divine calling and a royal appointment to rebuild the walls and secured their cooperation (Neh. 2:17). Despite the opposition of their neighbors, which escalated from mockery to attempted murder and included a plan to attack Jerusalem,[71] the walls were repaired in a mere fifty-two days (Neh. 6:15). Josephus, however, records that the project took two years and four months, a period of time some regard as more realistic.[72] Josephus' account is inconsistent,[73] however, and it is better to accept the Nehemiah version and assume that the walls were not as badly damaged as the report of Hanani and his associates would lead us to believe (Neh. 1:3).[74]   When the walls were repaired and the city gates restored, Nehemiah presided over a ceremony of dedication (Neh. 12:27-43).

Clearly, Nehemiah's major accomplishment was the rebuilding of the walls of Jerusalem. That, in fact, was the only assignment given him by Artaxerxes according to Neh. 2:4-8, but it appears from ch. 5 and elsewhere in the memoir[75] that, whether by original appointment or only be subsequent enlargement of his responsibility, Nehemiah discharged the full range of a governor's duties.[76]   He organized the guard for the gates (Neh. 7:1-3), took

---

[70] Chapter 2 says nothing about an appointment as governor, and most scholars believe that an initial limited appointment was later changed to a governorship. So Kellermann, *Nehemia*, p. 12; Ackroyd, *1 and 2 Chronicles, Ezra, Nehemiah*, pp. 284-85; Siegfried Herrmann, *A History of Israel in Old Testament Times*, 2nd ed., trans. John Bowden (Philadelphia, 1981), p. 313.

[71] Cf. Neh. 2:19; 3:33-4:17 (Ev. 4:1-23); 6:1-19.

[72] *Jewish Antiquities*, XI, 179. See e.g., Bright, *History*, p. 365.

[73] *Jewish Antiquities*, XI, 179 requires a date in the fifth month of the twenty-sixth year for the start of work on the wall, while XI, 168 puts it in the twenty-fifth year.

[74] Olmstead, *History*, p. 316.

[75] Neh. 7:1-3; 7:4 and 11:1-2; 13:4-31.

[76] Ackroyd, "Israel in the Exilic and Post-Exilic Periods," p. 335.

measures to increase the population of the city (Neh. 7:4; 11:1-2), and on several occasions dealt personally with internal problems of a social, political, or religious nature.

Nehemiah 5 describes Nehemiah's interventions on behalf of the poorer members of the community some of whom had lost their property or children to the more wealthy who had loaned them money at interest (Neh. 5:1-13). The context suggests that this happened while the work on the walls was in progress, and it has been suggested that the situation of the poor was exacerbated by their neglect of their regular occupations while they worked on the walls.[77] This is not impossible, but the text gives two reasons for their straits, famine and the tax exacted by the king, and does not mention the work on the wall, which for that matter only lasted fifty-two days. Further, 5:14-16 reflects on the entire twelve-year period that Nehemiah was in Jerusalem at any time during which the events of vv. 1-13 may have occurred.[78]

Nehemiah's mission to Judah was from the beginning regarded as a temporary assignment, and it is not surprising that after twelve years in 433 B.C.E. he returned to Artaxerxes in Susa (Neh. 13:6).[79] After a period of unspecified length, he returned to Jerusalem to find that in his absence serious abuses had been allowed, even perpetrated, by the priests and officials in Jerusalem. A large room within the temple precincts formerly used to store tithes and contributions given to the Levites, singers, gatekeepers and priests had been given to Tobiah by the priest Eliashib.[80] Not only was the storage room being misused, however, the tithes themselves had been discontinued, and the Levites and singers had abandoned their sacred duties in order to make a living. Enraged, Nehemiah acted with an authority that suggests he had been reappointed as governor. He threw out Tobiah's belongings, restored the room to its proper use, returned the dispersed Levites and singers to their posts, and harangued the officials on the importance of supporting the temple service (Neh. 13:4-14).

---

[77] Widengren, "The Persian Period," p. 531.

[78] Ackroyd, *1 and 2 Chronicles, Ezra, Nehemiah*, pp. 281-82.

[79] The evidence is inadequate to support Kellermann's theory that Nehemiah was recalled by Artaxerxes to stand trial. Cf. Kellermann, *Nehemia*, p. 203.

[80] Perhaps the high priest (cf. Neh. 3:1, 20; 13:28), but more likely another priest of the same name. Myers, *Ezra. Nehemiah*, p. 214.

There follow in chapter 13 two passages that appear to be additions to the memoir.[81]   The first gives us Nehemiah as an enforcer of strict Sabbath observance (Neh. 13:15-22), and in the second (Neh. 13:23-29) he prohibits intermarriage with foreigners and expels a grandson of the high priest who was married to the daughter of his nemesis Sanballat.

As to the further history of Nehemiah, how long he stayed in Judah, who succeeded him as governor, of this we know nothing. Only with the mission of Ezra in 398 B.C.E. do we again get a glimpse of the situation in Judah.

The Mission of Ezra

Later Judaism regarded the work of Ezra with great pride, and indeed the Chronicler treated it as the climax of his History Work.[82] Yet we must confess that we have little certain knowledge of Ezra or of his accomplishments. What we can know about these things must be derived for the most part from the Ezra Narrative (Ezra 7-10, Neh. 8-10), a text which is fraught with literary and chronological difficulties.

The Ezra material, it is widely recognized, bears all the marks of the Chronicler's style,[83] but this fact has led to very different conclusions. Thus Torrey argued that the Chronicler invented Ezra,[84] and Albright that the Chronicler was Ezra.[85] Kellermann, on the other hand, accepts the historicity of Ezra and the authenticity of his commission (Ezra 7:12-23, 25f.); the rest of the Ezra story, however, was in his view created by the Chronicler without benefit

---

[81] Note the connecting בימים ההמה at v. 15 and גם בימים ההם at v. 23 (cf. ההוא ביום at 12:44 and 13:1). Ackroyd, *1 and 2 Chronicles, Ezra, Nehemiah*, pp. 313-14, 317-20.

[82] Ackroyd, *1 and 2 Chronicles, Ezra, Nehemiah*, pp. 239-40.

[83] Cf. Kellermann, *Nehemia*, pp. 56-69. H.G.M. Williamson, *Israel in the Books of Chronicles* (Cambridge, 1977), and S. Japhet, "The Supposed Common Authorship of Chronicles and Ezra-Nehemiah Investigated Anew," *VT*, XVIII (1968), 330-71, take the opposite view.

[84] Torrey, *Ezra Studies*, pp. 238-48.

[85] W.F. Albright, "The Date and Personality of the Chronicler," *JBL*, XL (1921), 119-20. More recently Jacob Myers has espoused this view, cf. Myers, *Restoration*, p. 145.

of any source.[86]   Others assume that the Chronicler had a variety of sources for the Ezra Narrative, but that he exercised great freedom in his use of them.[87]

The chronology of Ezra's activities is also much debated.[88] That offered by the present arrangement of the text of Ezra and Nehemiah is extremely unlikely and has already been rejected. According to it Ezra would have preceded Nehemiah to Jerusalem in 458 B.C.E., settled the problem of foreign marriages almost immediately, and then waited more than a dozen years until after the arrival of Nehemiah in 445 to read the law. Contrary to this presentation, I have taken the position that the missions of Ezra and Nehemiah did not overlap, that Ezra followed Nehemiah to Jerusalem, and that only in its final stage did the Chronicler's History include the Nehemiah material. But even if all of this is correct, chronological difficulties remain. The most serious of these is that Ezra's resolution of the problem of mixed marriages, divorce "according to the law" (Ezra 10:3), precedes the reading of the law (Neh. 8) by at minimum the better part of a year.[89] Reluctantly, one comes to the conclusion that an understanding of the chronology of Ezra's activities will require a reordering of the text.[90]

Peter Ackroyd will allow the possibility that Ezra dissolved the foreign marriages before reading the law, but finds it more likely that two months after his arrival in the fifth month (Ezra 7:8-9), Ezra read the law in the seventh month ("which was traditionally associated with the reading of the law, cf. Deut. 31:10") and only then took action against the marriages which violated its stipulations.[91] The Chronicler, on this view, would have deferred the law reading ceremony in order to end his narrative on a high point with the climactic reading and accepting of the law followed by the celebration of Sukkoth, rather than on the chronologically correct

---

[86] Kellermann, *Nehemia*, pp. 56-69.

[87] Kurt Galling, "Bagoas und Esra," *Studien zur Geschichte Israels im persischen Zeitalter* (Tübingen, 1964), pp. 149-84; Ackroyd, *Israel Under Babylon and Persia*, pp. 263-64.

[88] Myers, *Ezra. Nehemiah*, pp. XLII-XLVIII, surveys a range of possibilities.

[89] Cf. Ezra 10:9; Neh. 8:2.

[90] Herrmann sees the difficulties, but cannot accept this conclusion. Cf. Herrmann, *History*, p. 309.

[91] Ackroyd, *1 and 2 Chronicles, Ezra, Nehemiah*, p. 251.

but depressing note of sending away something like one hundred wives and their children.[92]

Another line of approach reaches the same conclusion. By merely listing in chronological order the references in the Ezra story to days and months (without regard to their present narrative sequence and its implied chronological order), one arrives at a chronology that is plausible and which meets the objections raised by the present order of the materials. This chronology is as follows:[93]

1) First day of the first month (of the seventh year of Artaxerxes II, i.e. 398 B.C.E.), Ezra started preparing to go to Jerusalem (Ezra 7:9).

2) Twelfth day of the first month (same year), the company departed for Jerusalem (Ezra 8:31).

3) First day of the fifth month of the seventh year, the company arrived in Jerusalem (Ezra 7:8-9).

4) First day of the seventh month (same year), Ezra began to read from the law book (Neh. 8:2).

5) Twentieth day of the ninth month (same year), the people assembled in Jerusalem to deal with foreign marriages (Ezra 10:9).

6) First day of the tenth month (same year) to the first day of the first month (of the next year), the heads of houses dealt with foreign marriages individually (Ezra 10:16-17).

Based on this chronology the rearranged narrative sequence would be as follows:[94]

1) Ezra 7-8: Ezra's commission and the journey to Jerusalem.

---

[92] Ackroyd, *1 and 2 Chronicles, Ezra, Nehemiah*, p. 251.

[93] The following diverges only slightly from A. Gelin, *Le Livre de Esdras et Néhémie*, 2nd ed., La Sainte Bible (Paris, 1960), p. 14. Gelin puts the fast on the twenty-fourth day of "this month" (Neh. 9:1) after the divorce proceedings of Ezra 10. But Neh. 9:1 does not identify the month or the year and is meant in its context to refer to the seventh month. It may then refer to a Day of Atonement or, as Ackroyd, *1 and 2 Chronicles, Ezra, Nehemiah*, pp. 299-300, finds more likely, it may be an alternate tradition of the law reading ceremony. Myers, *Ezra. Nehemiah*, pp. XLIV-XLV, and *Restoration*, p. 137, follows Gelin exactly.

[94] Each of the three narrative units which follow has been interpolated.

   2)   Neh. 7:72-10:40 (Ev. 7:73-10:39): The reading of the law book followed by Sukkoth, a fast, and a covenant to support the temple.

   3)   Ezra 9-10: The problem of mixed marriages.

In what follows, I will attempt a description of the work of Ezra based on this sequence of events and the view that Ezra's commission was given in 398 B.C.E. But first a word of caution. All of our knowledge about Ezra and his work must be recognized as tentative. There is a consensus that he did exist and did have a mission to Jerusalem, but as we have seen not even that minimum is universally accepted. The date of his mission is one of the most debated issues in the history of biblical criticism, and although my evaluation of the limited evidence at our disposal has yielded the conclusion that 398 is more likely than 458 B.C.E., it has not done so by much. A good argument can be made for the opposite view. The texts on which we depend for our understanding of Ezra have been rewritten by the Chronicler, if not, as Kellermann believes, created by him. And those texts, of admittedly debatable historical value, must in my judgement be rearranged. To make matters worse, there are several plausible ways that can be done, each of which results in a different historical reconstruction.

In light of these difficulties one can appreciate Herrmann's decision to "follow the course of events as indicated by the arrangement of the sources in their present form, on the assumption that the redactors will not have confused the events completely."[95] As is clear by now, however, my own approach is to risk tentative decisions on these difficult issues and with due caution attempt a reconstruction of Ezra's period that can claim a greater likelihood of historicity than the Chronicler's account.

The story of Ezra begins abruptly in Ezra 7 with an incomplete genealogy the apparent purpose of which is to establish Ezra's priestly pedigree. But Ezra is also "a scribe (ספר) skilled in the law (תורה) of Moses" (Ezra 7:6), whom the king addressed as "the scribe (ספר) of the law (דתא) of the God of heaven" (v. 12). Schaeder's thesis that this phrase in v. 12 is an official Persian title meaning "*Referent für jüdische Religionsangelegenheiten*" has been strongly challenged and perhaps goes beyond the evidence.[96] It is

---

[95] Herrmann, *History*, p. 309.

[96] H.H. Schaeder, *Esra der Schreiber*, Beiträge zur historischen Theologie, V (Tübingen, 1930), pp. 39-59. Cf. Galling, "Bagoas und Esra," pp. 166-67; Ackroyd, *Israel Under Babylon and Persia*, pp. 267-68.

clear, nevertheless, that Ezra must have held a position of some importance to have had access to the king and to have been commissioned as he was. The commission itself may have been Ezra's idea[97] and was written by someone who was familiar with Jewish affairs and, presumably, an official whose job it was to deal with them. Who exactly it was we cannot know, but it is not impossible that it was Ezra himself.[98]

As in the case of Nehemiah, we should not assume that the Persian king's interest in Judah and willingness to send Jewish officials from his court to Jerusalem with funds to restore the community was based exclusively on his good nature. We will see that Ezra's assignment deals with internal Jewish affairs; but a stable and loyal Judah, especially since Egypt had just gained independence, was no doubt the end for which Artaxerxes hoped.[99]

Like Nehemiah Ezra was given a very specific mission. He was sent to Jerusalem "to make inquiries about Judah and Jerusalem according to the law of your God which is in your hand" (Ezra 7:14). He was also to transport the funds contributed by the king, his counselors and the Jews of Babylon for the support of the Jerusalem cult, as well as the sacred vessels (vv. 15-20). Finally, Ezra was to appoint magistrates and judges to judge those who knew the law, and was himself to teach those who did not (v. 25). The law was to be strictly enforced not only in Judah, but throughout the satrapy with violators severely punished (v. 25-26).

Two important questions immediately arise from the terms of Artaxerxes' decree. First, what is the precise meaning of the phrase in v. 14 "the law of your God which is in your hand"[100] (= "the wisdom of your God which is in your hand," v. 25)? And second, are we to understand that Ezra's authority to impose the law (v. 26) extends beyond Judah to the whole of the satrapy Beyond the River as v. 25 claims?

Scholars have almost universally assumed that Ezra literally had physical custody of a law book and was given the task of transporting it to Jerusalem where he was to introduce and enforce

---

[97] That was the Chronicler's view, cf. Ezra 7:6.

[98] Myers, *Ezra. Nehemiah*, pp. 60-62; Ackroyd, *1 and 2 Chronicles, Ezra, Nehemiah*, pp. 242-43.

[99] Cazelles, "La mission d'Esdras," p. 132.

[100] In particular, what is meant by בידך?

it.[101] In chapter 4 I will argue that, whatever actually happened, the Chronicler did not understand this text in that way. His view was that Ezra was a skilled interpreter of the law[102] (the book of which had for some time already been in Jerusalem) which the community should already know. For a long time it has been assumed that whatever the Chronicler affirmed (that could not be verified independently) should be rejected on the grounds that the Chronicler is always tendentious. Wellhausen referred, in fact, to such historical details as "paste pearls."[103] Nevertheless, it appears to me that the Chronicler has correctly understood his source. We note in the first place that nowhere in the commission is it suggested that the law in question is a law book, a written law or even a new law. The extraordinary and ubiquitous assumption that it was is based, presumably, on בידך in v. 14 and the fact that Ezra later read from the book of law at a public meeting, the results of which make clear that the people were not very familiar with the law's requirements (Neh. 8). I argue below that the use of בידך does not require the standard interpretation; in any case the commission itself rules out the notion that the law (whether a book or not) was new to the Jerusalem community. Ezra's commission is hardly to impose a new law on the Judeans from outside. Rather, the king sent him to Judah to investigate the degree of compliance with the known law, to arrange for its strict enforcement, and to instruct any who are ignorant of it (vv. 14, 25-26).

This interpretation has the added virtue of not conflicting with what we know of Persian policies with regard to subject peoples in general and the Jews in particular. There is, we must never forget, much that we cannot at present know about the history of the Persian period, but all the evidence we have suggests that the imposition of a new law on a subject people was opposite to the Persian strategy. To do so in Judah in 398 B.C.E. (or 458 for that matter) would almost certainly create rebellion and incite a movement for religious (and national) freedom.

Similar considerations suggest the answer to the other question posed above. Was Ezra empowered to enforce Jewish law in the entire satrapy Beyond the River? Certainly not. Such power could

---

[101] Blenkinsopp, "Sectarianism," p. 5, and L.H. Brockington, *Ezra, Nehemiah and Esther*, The Century Bible (London, 1969), p. 92, take exception to this consensus.

[102] Taking בידך metaphorically, cf. below pp. 73-74.

[103] Wellhausen, *Prolegomena*, p. 224.

do the Persians no good and would cause much unrest. The claim in v. 25 that Ezra had this authority is, as Morton Smith points out, an addition to the text based on "wishful thinking."[104]

Ezra's commission is not dated, but cannot have been far removed from the first day of the first month of 398 B.C.E., at which time Ezra began his preparations for the trip to Jerusalem (v. 9). Artaxerxes had given the exiles permission to emigrate to Judah (v. 13) and a number joined Ezra. The company assembled at Ahava where, we are told, Ezra discovered that not one of the roughly fifteen hundred men[105] was a Levite (8:15). Ezra remedied this unacceptable circumstance by sending to "the place Casiphia" (twice in v. 17) from which some forty-one Levites and two-hundred-twenty temple servants (נתינים) were recruited (vv. 17-20). This passage stresses the Chronicler's interest in the Levites and the necessity of their functions so neatly that one has to doubt its historicity. If it did not happen, however, it is still a note of particular historical interest since it implies a Jewish temple in Babylon.[106]

On the twelfth day of the first month the rounded-out party began their journey. They arrived in Jerusalem, having been protected by God along the way, about three and one-half months later (Ezra 8:31; 7:8-9). Ezra quickly transferred the valuables he had conveyed from Babylon to a group headed by the priest Meremoth. This was done in the temple in a most businesslike manner (Ezra 8:32-34).

Two months later, on the first day of the seventh month, Ezra began to read the law book at a great outdoor convocation (Neh. 8:2-4).[107] The next day the leaders of the community gathered for further study of the book and discovered therein the requirements for the feast of Sukkoth which was then kept ככתוב (Neh. 8:13-18). Following this, "on the twenty-fourth day of this month" (Neh. 9:1), the assembly held a day of fasting during which they confessed their sins and read from the law (Neh. 9:1-5). At least so

---

[104] Morton Smith, *Palestinian Parties and Politics That Shaped the Old Testament* (New York and London, 1971), p. 197.

[105] The number five thousand in Widengren, "The Persian Period," p. 535, must include an estimate of the number of women and children.

[106] Cf. Ackroyd, *1 and 2 Chronicles, Ezra, Nehemiah*, p. 248.

[107] This text is discussed below, cf. pp. 83-84, 100-103.

the Chronicler says. But the historicity of this ceremony[108] and its relationship to the previous events in the seventh month are difficult to determine. If Sukkoth was kept from the fifteenth to the twenty-second of the month,[109] then this fast two days later appears closely connected. There are, however, some reasons to question whether the tradition in 9:1-5 is not actually a variant account of the law reading ceremony presented by the Chronicler as a prior event in ch. 8.[110]

The next and last important event in the mission of Ezra of which we have knowledge began to unfold about two months after Sukkoth when Shecaniah together with "those who trembled at the commandment of our God" proposed a radical solution to the problem of foreign marriages, namely divorce. That is, they proposed "a covenant with God to put away all these wives and their children...כתורה" (Ezra 10:2-4).[111]   Not surprisingly this was acceptable to Ezra, and the entire male population of the Golah was ordered to Jerusalem on pain of expropriation of their property and exclusion from the community (Ezra 10:7-9). Once there the crowd sat in a downpour while Ezra accused them of marrying foreign women and ordered them to separate from "the people of the land and from the foreign wives" (Ezra 10:9-11). The people were willing to do this, but because of the rain and the number of marriages involved it was decided that the leaders of the people would meet to deal with the marriages on an individual basis, a task which was to occupy them for the next two months (Ezra 10:12-17).

One can hardly overestimate the bitterness that this exclusivity must have caused between the Golah community and the people of the land. There is in fact evidence that it caused some dissent within the Golah itself (Ezra 10:15).[112]   This points out an important aspect of the whole restoration period, namely what Joseph Blenkinsopp calls "the tendency to sectarianism."[113]

While Kellermann's identification in Nehemiah's time of well-defined Zionist and theocratic parties locked in conflict probably

---

[108] This day of fasting and repentance is the closest the Chronicler comes to describing the Day of Atonement (cf. Lev. 16; Num. 29: 7-11).

[109] These are the dates the Chronicler required, cf. below, pp. 99, 103.

[110] Cf. below, p. 84.

[111] No text in the Hebrew Bible requires this.

[112] The text, however, does not make clear the dissidents' objections.

[113] Blenkinsopp, "Sectarianism."

goes too far,[114] it is clear that there were sharp divisions in the community, especially regarding the requirements of membership in it.[115]   Thus, notwithstanding that they are no doubt Yahwists, Sanballat and Tobiah are told by Nehemiah that they have no portion in Jerusalem (Neh. 2:20),[116] and Nehemiah, as we have seen, was thought to have been violently opposed to marriages with foreigners, among whom were included Sanballat and his family (Neh. 13:23-29). These divisions within the community, which in Blenkinsopp's view foreshadow the emergence of later sects, were based on rival claims as to the contents and meaning of the law.[117]

Summary and Conclusion

From the very beginning, with the decree of Cyrus in 539 B.C.E., the Persians pursued a political policy of toleration and even support of the religions of the captive peoples. This policy was intended to encourage loyalty and forestall nationalistic revolt. No doubt it was generally successful.

It is in the context of this policy that the Persian support for the Judean restoration can be best understood. The decree of Cyrus, Darius' support of the rebuilding of the temple, and the commissions of Nehemiah and Ezra all benefited the Jews, but were intended to benefit the Persians by stabilizing the West.

To some extent, however, the missions of Nehemiah (445 B.C.E.) and Ezra (cautiously dated 398 B.C.E.) destabilized Judah by dividing the populace on issues such as the requirements for membership in the community and the contents, authority, and interpretation of the written torah. The Chronicler's History Work with its many assertions about what exactly the law required represents one side in this long debate.

---

[114] Kellermann, *Nehemia*, pp. 174-76; cf. Ackroyd, "Israel in the Exilic and Post-Exilic Periods," p. 335.

[115] Blenkinsopp, "Sectarianism," pp. 7, 11-13.

[116] Tobiah is a Yahwistic name as are the names of Sanballat's sons (Delaiah and Shelemaiah). Cf. Ackroyd, *1 and 2 Chronicles, Ezra, Nehemiah*, p. 272.

[117] Blenkinsopp, "Sectarianism," pp. 5, 7-8.

Chapter 3

Sources and the Problem of Authorship in the Chronicler's History Work

That the Books of Chronicles, Ezra and Nehemiah are to a large extent based on sources has never been disputed. Neither is there any doubt that parts of them are secondary. There is little agreement, however, among students of these books as to the exact nature and extent of these underlying sources, and identifying which passages are secondary is likewise an occasion for considerable disagreement. Indeed, as we shall see, there have been a number of recent attempts to describe the redactional history of Chronicles, Ezra and Nehemiah. Unfortunately, these efforts have not led to a consensus.

In this chapter I will enumerate the major sources on which the present books of Chronicles, Ezra and Nehemiah depend and then examine in some detail the recent efforts to deny the very widely held view that the books are essentially a single work. A discussion of major recent theories of the books' redactional history will follow, and although it will not be possible to argue the position in detail, I will define what I mean by the Chronicler's History Work. The chapter will conclude with a necessarily brief treatment of the date of the Chronicler's History.

The Sources of Chronicles and Ezra-Nehemiah

Throughout the Books of Chronicles one finds references to the sources on which the books purportedly are based.[1]   Among these supposed sources is a midrash on the book of kings (המלכים

---

[1] Cf. Jacob M. Myers, *1 Chronicles. Introduction, Translation, and Notes*, The Anchor Bible XII (Garden City, 1965), pp. XLV-XLVIII, for a complete list.

41

מדרש ספר, 2 Chron. 24:27). This citation, taken with the fact that for all their obvious similarities the Books of Chronicles diverge, in some places remarkably, from Samuel--Kings, has led to the theory that the Chronicler did not use Samuel--Kings but used instead a Midrash of them from which at least some of the material in Chronicles not found in the former derives.[2]   An analysis of these citations reveals, however, that their location in the text corresponds to the similar citations found in the books of Samuel--Kings.[3] What is remarkable in this regard, as Williamson points out, is that the source citation in three instances does not come in its usual place at the end of the account of the king's reign but shortly before, exactly as it does in the Kings account of these reigns.[4]

   If it is quite likely, then, that the primary source for the Books of Chronicles was the Deuteronomistic Historian's narrative in Samuel and Kings, it is still the case that much in Chronicles is not found in the *Vorlage*, and where there are synoptic passages, differences in detail are common. While this latter point was once understood as evidence of the assumed Midrash or an indication of the Chronicler's biases, it is now virtually certain that in at least some cases it reflects the Chronicler's use of a text of Samuel--Kings other than the MT.[5]

   The Chronicler's genealogies suggest, and his references to legal material demonstrate, that in addition to the Deuteronomistic History, material now in the Pentateuch was also known to the Chronicler.[6]   There are a number of passages in Chronicles, however, for which we have no independently preserved sources. These must be dealt with individually, although to do so here would contribute little to the subject of this investigation. Some of these

---

[2] Eissfeldt, *The Old Testament*, pp. 531-35, argues this position.

[3] 1 Chron. 29:29 and 2 Chron. 35:26-27 are the only exceptions. The former is the Chronicler's creation, and the latter is based on 2 Kgs. 23:28.

[4] Cf. 2 Chron. 16:11 (1 Kgs. 15:23), 2 Chron. 20:34 (1 Kgs. 22:45), 2 Chron. 25:26 (2 Kgs. 14:18), and H.G.M. Williamson, *1 and 2 Chronicles*, The New Century Bible Commentary (Grand Rapids and London, 1982), p. 18.

[5] Eugene Charles Ulrich, Jr., *The Qumran Text of Samuel and Josephus*, Harvard Semitic Monographs, ed. Frank Moore Cross, Jr., XIX (Missoula, 1978), pp. 151-64; Werner E. Lemke, "The Synoptic Problem in the Chronicler's History," *Harvard Theological Review*, LVIII (1965), 349-63; J.T. Milik, *Ten Years of Discovery in the Wilderness of Judea*, trans. J. Strugnell (Naperville, 1959), p. 25.

[6] Cf. Ch. 5.

texts are no doubt the Chronicler's free composition, but others certainly depended on sources lost to us.

The question of sources in Ezra and Nehemiah is much more difficult. It is clear that some sources were used, but since none have survived apart from the books of Ezra and Nehemiah, it is not possible to be certain in every case whether a particular text is a free composition, an extensively rewritten source or a source simply incorporated into the larger work. Again, an exhaustive source analysis is not the subject of this work. There are a few points of general agreement, however, which should be mentioned.

One such point, and the least controversial, is the view that a Nehemiah source was incorporated essentially without change into the present work. It is by no means certain, however, as we shall see, that the Nehemiah material should be regarded as a source of the Chronicler's Work rather than an addition to it.

Somewhat more debated is the question of the source of the Ezra Narrative. Most scholars assume that the Chronicler had a source or sources for this, but the material in its present form is so typical of his style that one must assume the source(s) to have been thoroughly rewritten.[7] The alternative, which Torrey and to a lesser extent Kellermann support, is to take the view that the Chronicler composed the Ezra story without recourse to sources other than his imagination and the needs of his theology.[8]

Finally there is the matter of the Aramaic sections in Ezra (4:8-6:18, 7:12-26), regarding which there are two main issues. First, do they represent a source or sources or were they created by the Chronicler? And second, what is their historical value? Although related these questions must be distinguished. While a decision that the Chronicler invented the Aramaic documents suggests the answer to the question of their historical reliability, the reverse is not true. The material could derive from a source and yet not be trustworthy. In any case, our concern here is with the question of sources and not of their reliability. A minority of scholars have held that the Aramaic material was the Chronicler's creation,[9] but most take the view either that the Chronicler had a number of sources in Aramaic[10] or

---

[7] Cf. e.g., Myers, *Ezra. Nehemiah*, pp. L-LI.

[8] Torrey, *Ezra Studies*, pp. 238-48; Kellermann, *Nehemia*, pp. 56-69, allows the possibility that the Chronicler had a source for Ezra 7:12-23, 26, and 8:26-27.

[9] Torrey, *Ezra Studies*, pp. 238-48; Kellermann, *Nehemia*, pp. 56-69.

[10] E.g., Myers, *Ezra. Nehemiah*, pp. XLVIII-LI.

that the various Aramaic pericopes came to the Chronicler already combined as a single source.[11]

As vexing as the detailed questions of the nature, extent and use of sources in the books of Chronicles, Ezra and Nehemiah are, the problem of their combination into an extended History Work is greater. Do the present Chronicles, Ezra and Nehemiah constitute an original unity? Were they always separate as in the MT? Or was there some redactional stage at which they became a unity? How, finally, did the sources combine and what, in light of these difficulties, is meant by the Chronicler's History Work? It is to these questions that we now turn.

The Problem of Authorship in Chronicles and Ezra-Nehemiah

The dominant and until very recently virtually unchallenged consensus of Old Testament scholarship is the view implied in the Talmud,[12] first argued by L. Zunz,[13] and repeated with only minor variations in almost every Introduction and Commentary since,[14] namely: notwithstanding the numerous short interpolations of a later hand, the present Books of Chronicles, Ezra and Nehemiah are essentially the literary product of a single author.

The evidence everywhere adduced in support of this conclusion is as follows:

1. The Books of Chronicles, Ezra, and Nehemiah evidence to a remarkable degree the same peculiarities of vocabulary, style, point of view, and theology.
2. The end of 2 Chronicles and the beginning of Ezra are virtually identical.
3. The masora at the end of Nehemiah includes Ezra, which itself is not followed by the standard massoretic notices.
4. I Esdras begins with 2 Chron. 35 and continues without interruption or repetition with the Ezra narrative including Neh. 8.

---

[11] Bowman, *Ezra and Nehemiah*, p. 557; Ackroyd, *1 and 2 Chronicles, Ezra, Nehemiah*, p. 227.

[12] b. Baba Bathra 15a.

[13] L. Zunz, *Die gottesdienstlichen Vorträge der Juden historisch entwickelt* (Berlin, 1832), pp. 13-36.

[14] Cf. Williamson, *Israel*, p. 5 n. 3, for a list of scholars who have disassociated themselves from this consensus.

Despite this evidence and the almost univocal assertions of scholars since Zunz, the issue at present is far from being resolved. That such is the case is an indication of the strength of the recent challenge mounted against the consensus. It will be necessary to consider in some detail the counter arguments, and to determine to the extent that the evidence will allow the unity or extent of the Chronicler's Work; only then can we proceed to an investigation of its relationship to pentateuchal legislation.

The Critique of the Consensus

While there have always been a few who rejected the majority opinion, the recent assault on the consensus view of unity of authorship in Chronicles, Ezra, and Nehemiah can be traced to D.N. Freedman's essay of 1961.[15] The essay is an attempt to shed light on the problem of the Chronicler's intentions, that is, his purpose for composing his extended history of Israel. The standard way to discover this has been to note in detail how the Chronicler modified his deuteronomistic source, and yields the conclusion that the Chronicler's purpose was to present Israel's history in the light of Priestly legislation, that is, as if the P code had been in effect.[16] Freedman, however, reads the Chronicler's purpose off the surface of the narrative, without reference to its sources, and concludes that his purpose was to write a history of David and Solomon which would legitimate the restoration of the Davidic dynasty and its authority in the cult in the period of Sheshbazzar and Zerubbabel (ca. 515 B.C.E.).[17] Because Freedman finds this purpose lacking in Ezra-Nehemiah, which bases the restoration on Mosaic rather than Davidic authority, he must conclude that the Chronicler's Work did not originally extend beyond the period of Zerubbabel's rebuilding of the temple, that is, Ezra 3:13.[18] In his view, then, the conclusion of the Chronicler's work has been replaced by the

---

[15] D.N. Freedman, "The Chronicler's Purpose," *CBQ*, XXIII (1961), pp. 436-42.

[16] Cf. e.g., Eissfeldt, *The Old Testament*, p. 539.

[17] Freedman, "Purpose," pp. 440-41.

[18] Freedman, "Purpose," p. 441. We will see below that this is a false dichotomy. Chronicles and Ezra-Nehemiah both cite Mosaic and Davidic authority.

originally independent memoirs of Ezra and Nehemiah.[19]   The flaw in this whole line of reasoning is his failure to take adequate account of the nature of the Chronicler's History, whatever its original extent, as a source-based work.   Since the differences between the Books of Chronicles and Ezra-Nehemiah which Freedman identifies also existed in the sources of Chronicles and Ezra-Nehemiah, the conclusion that the latter was therefore not originally a part of the Chronicler's Work begs the question.

Freedman's arguments were, nevertheless, accepted by F.M. Cross, who in a masterful and persuasive essay argued that Freedman's original Chronicler's Work of ca. 515 B.C.E. was the first of three major editions.[20]   An original version (1 Chron. 10-2 Chron. 34 plus the *Vorlage* of 1 Esdras 1:1-5:65), a second edition which includes the rest of the *Vorlage* of 1 Esdras, and a final version which contains 1 Chron. 1-9 and the Hebrew Ezra and Nehemiah. This conclusion is the result of a long and complicated line of thought, the major presupposition of which is the practice of papponymy in the high priestly family in the period of the restoration.

Cross begins by noting the significance of the as yet unpublished Dâliyeh papyri for reconstructing the sequence of Samaritan governors. He had previously argued that the Sanballat referred to in Dâliyeh papyri numbers five and fourteen must be dated ca. 375 B.C.E. and thus cannot be the fifth century Sanballat (I) of the Bible and the Elephantine papyri or the Sanballat associated by Josephus with Darius III and Alexander.[21]   Prior to the discovery of a Sanballat in the Dâliyeh material, Cross allows that it seemed likely that Josephus had simply assigned erroneous dates to Sanballat, who was correctly located by the biblical references in the period of Nehemiah. With conclusive proof of a second Sanballat provided by the Dâliyeh papyri, however, Cross insists that the possibility of a third, that of Josephus, can no longer

---

[19] Freedman, "Purpose," p. 441.

[20] F.M. Cross, "A Reconstruction of the Judean Restoration," *JBL*, XCIV (1975), 4-18. Cross prefers to date the first version to 520 B.C.E., regarding it as an anticipation of the rebuilding of the temple, pp. 13-14.

[21] F.M. Cross, "Papyri of the Fourth Century B.C. from Dâliyeh," in D.N. Freedman and J. Greenfield eds., *New Directions in Biblical Archeology* (New York, 1969), pp. 42-44, 53-57, and F.M. Cross, "The Discovery of the Samaria Papyri," *BA*, XXVI (1963), p. 121, Cf. *AP* 30:18, 29 and Josephus, *Antiquities* XI, 302-303, 306-12, 325.

be ruled out.[22]   This then constitutes proof for Cross that like the Tobiads and the Ammonites the Samaritan ruling house practiced papponymy.[23]   Cross asserts that "the sequence of Saballatids makes certain what has long been suspected, that two generations are missing in the biblical genealogy of Jewish high priests."[24] These, he maintains, are the Johanan and Jaddua that Josephus correctly, according to Cross, associated with the period of Artaxerxes III and Alexander,[25] and who were the grandsons respectively of the Johanan and Jaddua of the biblical lists.[26]   The two names are omitted from the biblical lists according to Cross, by a "simple haplography...in extremely easy consequence of the device of papponymy."[27]

With the addition of a second Johanan and Jaddua, the genealogy of priests from the sixth to the fourth centuries records ten generations over a span, by Cross' reckoning, of 275 years; and yields the figure of 27.5 years per generation. On the basis of the Davidic genealogy which yields an average of 24.5 years per generation, Cross finds the figure of 27.5 "suspiciously high."[28] Suspecting another haplography, Cross notes that both Johanan and Joiada are identified as the son of Eliashib.[29]   This suggests to Cross that a second Eliashib and Johanan, like Johanan and Jaddua after them, have been omitted by haplography.[30]

Cross is then able to provide a reconstructed genealogy of the high priests as follows:[31]
1.   Jehozadak. Born before 587, the father of- (1 Chron. 5:41; Ev. 6:15)
2.   Jeshua. Born ca. 570, the father of- (Neh. 12:10)

---

[22] Cross, "Papyri of the Fourth Century," pp. 55-56.

[23] Cross, "Papyri of the Fourth Century," pp. 55-56; cf. Cross, "Samaria Papyri," pp. 120-21, and "A Reconstruction," pp. 6-7.

[24] Cross, "A Reconstruction," p. 5.

[25] Josephus, *Antiquities* XI, 302-303, 306-12, 347.

[26] Neh. 12:10-11, 22.

[27] Cross, "A Reconstruction," p. 6.

[28] Cross, "A Reconstruction," p. 9.

[29] Cp. Ezra 10:6 and Neh. 12:23 with Neh. 12:10, 22.

[30] Cross, "A Reconstruction," p. 10.

[31] Cf. Cross, "A Reconstruction," p. 17.

3.   Joiakim. Born ca. 545, the (brother)[32] of- (Neh. 12:10)
3.   Eliashib (I). Born ca. 545, the father of- (Not in the list of Neh. 12, but restored by Cross on the basis of Neh. 12:23 and Ezra 10:6, which speak of an Eliashib whose son was Johanan. According to Neh. 12:10-11, 22 Eliashib's son was Joiada and Johanan was his grandson).
4.   Johanan (I). Born ca. 520, the father of- (supplied by Cross for the same reason as the immediately foregoing).
5.   Eliashib (II). Born ca. 495, the father of- (Neh. 12:10, 22).
6.   Joiada [33] (I). Born ca. 470, the father of (Neh. 12:11, 22).
7.   Johanan (II). Born ca. 445, the father of- (Neh. 12:11, 22).
8.   Jaddua [34] (II). Born ca. 420, the father of- (Neh. 12:11).
9.   Johanan (III). Born ca. 395, the father of- (Not in the biblical lists; restored by Cross on the basis of Josephus, *Ant.* XI, 297-303).
10. Jaddua (III). Born ca. 370, the father of- (Supplied by Cross for the same reason as the immediately foregoing).
11. Onias (I) (=Johanan IV).[35] Born ca. 345, the father of- (*Ant.* XI, 347).
12. Simon (I). Born ca. 320.

On the basis of this genealogy and the text of Ezra 10:6, which identifies Jehohanan (=Johanan I) the son of Eliashib as Ezra's contemporary, Cross is able to place the date of Ezra's mission in the seventh year of Artaxerxes I, that is 458 B.C.E.[36]

Taken together with the evidence of 1 Esdras (see below), the reconstructed genealogy of the high priests also provides Cross with

---

[32] Although identified as the father of Eliashib at Neh. 12:10, Cross, for chronological reasons, holds that Joiakim was his brother. Cf. Cross, "A Reconstruction," p. 10 n. 39.

[33] Cross thinks that Eliashib (II) had an older son named Johanan, who for some reason did not become high priest. Cross, "A Reconstruction," p. 10 n. 38.

[34] Jaddua is a caritative of Joiada. Cross, "A Reconstruction," p. 6 n. 12.

[35] Onias is the Greek form of Hebrew Honay, the caritative of Yohanan. Cross, "A Reconstruction," p. 6 n. 12.

[36] Cross, "A Reconstruction," p. 11.

the key to the editorial history of the Books of Chronicles, Ezra, and Nehemiah. In 1 Esdras the Ezra narrative (including Neh. 7:72b-8:12) is presented in order and entirely without reference to Nehemiah or his memoirs. From this Cross concludes that an earlier edition of the Chronicler's Work ended with the original conclusion of 1 Esdras 9, and thus did not include the Nehemiah Memoir, which was circulated independently.[37] This conclusion is verified, he maintains, by the fact that Josephus is following a text of 1 Esdras which concludes with the Feast of Tabernacles.[38] Final confirmation of the existence of this earlier recension is found in Neh. 12:23, which refers to ספר דברי הימים ("The Book of Chronicles") in which a levitical genealogy is recorded "until the days of Johanan the son of Eliashib."[39] This Cross takes to be a reference to an edition of the Chronicler's Work which extended to the period of Ezra's contemporary, Johanan the son of Eliashib, but does not continue to the period of Nehemiah and his contemporary, Eliashib II the son of Johanan I.

With this evidence of two editions and Freedman's arguments for an original version which corresponds with neither of them, Cross is now prepared to speak of the three editions of the Chronicler's History Work: Chr 1, Chr 2, Chr 3.

Chr 1 is the original version as identified by Freedman. It consisted of 1 Chronicles 10-2 Chronicles 34 plus the *Vorlage* of 1 Esdras 1:1-5:65 (=2 Chron. 34:1 through Ezra 3:13). This was a piece of pro-Zerubbabel propaganda and was composed ca. 520.[40] To this was added the rest of the *Vorlage* of 1 Esdras. This is Chr 2, the recension referred to at Neh. 12:23. Finally, Chr 3 added the genealogies of 1 Chron. 1-9 and the Hebrew Ezra-Nehemiah, which was composed by incorporating the memoirs of Nehemiah into the Ezra narrative.[41] These subsequent editions, moreover, can be dated by correlating their genealogical notices with Cross's reconstructed list. The latest high priest referred to in Chr 2 is Ezra's contemporary Johanan the son of Eliashib (1 Esdras 9:1 = Ezra 10:6). The last Davidid is Hattush (1 Esdras 8:29 = Ezra 8:2). In Chr 3, however, the Davidic genealogy continues for two

---

[37] Cross, "A Reconstruction," pp. 7-9.
[38] Cross, "A Reconstruction," pp. 8-9. *Ant.* XI, 1-158.
[39] Cross, "A Reconstruction," p. 11.
[40] Cross, "A Reconstruction," pp. 12-14.
[41] Cross, "A Reconstruction," p. 13.

generations to Anani (1 Chron. 3:24) who was a contemporary of
Johanan II and probably also Jaddua II, who are mentioned
elsewhere in Chr 3.[42] On this basis Cross dates Chr 2 at ca. 450
and Chr 3 ca. 400 B.C.E.[43]

Cross has clearly provided us with a magnificent *tour de force*,
which appears to resolve major longstanding problems of Chronicler
research. The mission of Ezra can now be dated confidently at 458,
and the editorial history of the present Books of Chronicles, Ezra
and Nehemiah is finally described. Unfortunately, closer
examination of Cross's presuppositions and the details of his
argument reveals that these problems remain as intractable as ever.

As Cross makes clear, the key to his solutions lies in the
reconstructed list of the Jewish high priests in the period of the
restoration. The basic presupposition underlying the reconstruction
that Cross offers is that the high priests practiced papponymy from
the beginning of the sixth century down to the Greek period. The
grounds for supposing this is that papponymy was widely practiced
in ruling families of contemporary neighboring peoples.[44] But
while it is true that the Tobiads and Oniads practiced papponymy
regularly, neither the governors of Judah nor the Davidids used
papponymy at all, and there is little evidence of papponymy in the
list of high priests prior to the Greek period.

Cross, however, would claim that even without his additions,
the biblical genealogy of high priests itself reveals the practice of
papponymy. In fact, however, in a list of nine names over eight
generations (i.e., Jehozadak, Jeshua, Joiakim, Eliashib, Joiada,
Johanan, Jaddua [=Joiada], Onias [= Johanan], Simon) papponymy
occurs but twice.[45] Moreover, even with his emendations, which
are based on assumed haplographies which are entirely without
textual evidence, Cross's reconstructed list exhibits papponymy
only five times in twelve generations.[46] Thus only Eliashib II,
Jaddua II, Johanan III, Jaddua III, and Onias I are named after their
respective grandfathers. Of these five occurrences three are the

---

[42] E.g., Neh. 12:11, 22.

[43] Cross, "A Reconstruction," pp. 11-14.

[44] Cross, "A Reconstruction," pp. 5-6.

[45] Jaddua is a caritative of Joiada, and Onias of Johanan. Cross, "A
Reconstruction," p. 6, n. 12.

[46] Really thirteen generations since Eliashib is the son (not brother) of Joiakim.
Cf. Neh. 12:10.

product of Cross's emendations.

As the assumption of papponymy is the key to Cross's list of high priests, the assumption of a twenty-five year average generation for the high priests is the key to his chronology. Cross arrives at this figure on the basis of the genealogy of the Davidids.[47] Although Cross does not mention it, this genealogy too is based on a textual emendation, in this case of 1 Chron. 3:22. Cross appears, here as elsewhere in his article, to be following Albright who argued that "and the sons of Shemai'ah" in 1 Chron. 3:22 "is proved by the rest of the verse to be an error of a copyist."[48] The real problem with this reasoning, however, is that, even if the average Davidic generation spanned twenty-five years, we cannot be confident that the same was true of the high priests.[49]

The basis on which Cross adds a second Eliashib and Johanan, besides the requirements of a chronology based on twenty-five year generations, is the "juxtaposition of the priests Johanan son of Eliashib and Joiada son of Eliashib."[50] From this Cross concludes that there were two Eliashibs and, "given papponymy," two Johanans. Several other explanations are possible. The most likely are that a copyist erred, that Joiada and Johanan were brothers, or that בן at Ezra 10:6 and Neh. 12:23 means "grandson."[51]

One of the consequences of adding a second Eliashib and Johanan in the sequence from Jehozadak to Johanan is that the average generation would be 21.4 years.[52] This is too few by Cross's reckoning. Therefore Eliashib is made the brother of Joiakim[53] (despite the fact that Neh. 12:10 identifies him as the son), thereby reducing the number of generations by one and

---

[47] See the chart in Cross, "A Reconstruction," p. 17, and p. 9.

[48] Albright, "Personality," p. 110 n. 15.

[49] Widengren, "The Persian Period," pp. 508-509.

[50] Cross, "A Reconstruction," p. 10. Cp. Ezra 10:6 and Neh. 12:23 with Neh. 12:10, 22.

[51] So Albright seems to take it. Cf. Albright,*The Biblical Period*, p. 94.

[52] Cross figures 150 years from the birth of Jehozadak (ca. 595 B.C.E.) to the birth of Johanan (ca. 445 B.C.E.). Cross, "A Reconstruction," p. 10 and n. 32. With the addition we have eight names, seven generations, over 150 years, i.e. 21.4 years per generation.

[53] Cross, "A Reconstruction," p. 10 n. 39.

resulting in an average generation of twenty-five years, exactly the figure Cross is looking for.

A second consequence of the addition of an Eliashib and a Johanan is the need to explain why Eliashib II's son is named Joiada instead of Johanan as the practice of papponymy (and the hypothetical haplography of Eliashib II and Johanan II) would require. Cross's suggestion that Joiada is the brother of Eliashib's eldest son, Johanan, who for some reason did not become high priest[54] is certainly possible. Unfortunately, our sources are completely silent about such a person.

Cross finds in the narratives of 1 Esdras and Josephus conclusive evidence that an earlier version of the Chronicler's Work (Chr 2) circulated without the Nehemiah Memoir. The evidence of 1 Esdras and of Josephus, however, is not unambiguous as we will see below. Let it suffice for the present to note that it is not clear whether 1 Esdras reflects an earlier version of our Chronicles-Ezra-Nehemiah (as Cross assumes) or is a secondary work, based on-- and attempting to resolve the literary problems of--our Ezra-Nehemiah. As for Josephus, while it is apparent that he is following 1 Esdras, if 1 Esdras is secondary, then his account can shed no light on earlier editions of Chronicles-Ezra-Nehemiah.

The genealogical references on which Cross depends are also fragile. Such lists are easily interpolated or lengthened, and such additions are difficult to discover. Moreover, Neh. 12:23 may refer to a source rather than an edition of the Chronicler's Work.[55] And, of course, if we are not persuaded by Cross's reconstructed list of high priests, then we cannot accept his editions (and their dates) which are based on it.

The most plausible part of Cross's reconstruction is the addition to the biblical lists of the Johanan and Jaddua associated by Josephus with a Sanballat from the period of Darius III and Alexander. While Josephus confused this Sanballat with the Sanballat of the Bible, the existence of a second Sanballat is proved by the Dâliyeh papyri, which makes it seem more likely that a third, that of Josephus, also existed. The rest of Cross's theory is more problematic. It depends too much on emendations which are without textual evidence and explanations drawn from silence; most importantly, it is unnecessary. The biblical genealogy of high

---

[54] Cross, "A Reconstruction," p. 10 n. 38.
[55] Myers, *Ezra. Nehemiah* , p. 199, and Batten, *The Books of Ezra and Nehemiah*, pp. 24, 277.

priests suggests an average generation of from thirty to thirty-five years. If such a figure was accepted, and that is not so difficult as Cross assumes, then Eliashib would have been born about 500 B.C.E., which would make him about fifty-five when Nehemiah came to Jerusalem in 445. Johanan, his grandson, would have been born ca. 440, and would thus be about forty-two when Ezra came in 398 B.C.E.[56]

The first direct challenge to the consensus view that the Books of Chronicles, Ezra and Nehemiah were an original unity and the product of a single author was mounted by Sara Japhet.[57] Hers is a detailed and narrowly-focused rebuttal of the assertion that Chronicles and Ezra-Nehemiah in their grammatical, syntactical and stylistic similarities evidence a common author. Using such rubrics as "Linguistic Opposition," "Specific Technical Terms," and "Peculiarities of Style," Japhet marshals the evidence which to her mind mandates the inescapable conclusion that the Books of Chronicles and Ezra-Nehemiah "could not have been written or compiled by the same author."[58]

Japhet's work is careful and thorough, and her evidence is impressive; our question, however, is whether the evidence requires the conclusion she draws. If the Books of Chronicles and Ezra-Nehemiah were available to us as original, unedited literary wholes and were found to display the differences that Japhet cites, her argument would be enhanced. It is the assumption that we have such documents to investigate which lends the appearance of certitude to her conclusion. In fact, the present Books of Chronicles and Ezra-Nehemiah bear all the marks of a source-based composition which has undergone extensive editing and subsequent expansion. What is not yet clear is the extent to which Japhet's evidence exhibits original differences as opposed to those which derive from subsequent editorial activity.

On the other hand, the relationship of the Chronicler's Work (especially in Ezra-Nehemiah) to its sources is still obscure and makes an investigation such as Japhet's much more problematic than she seems to recognize. In the first place, if the Chronicler depended for the Books of Chronicles on Samuel-Kings (and not on a Midrash of them), it is still the case that he did not follow the MT

---

[56] Widengren, "The Persian Period," pp. 508-509.

[57] Japhet, "Authorship," pp. 330-71.

[58] Japhet, "Authorship," p. 371.

or even the Proto-MT of them.[59]   Yet Japhet's comparison assumes
he did.   In Ezra-Nehemiah the identification of the Chronicler's
sources is difficult, and because they do not exist independently an
analysis of his use of them is all but impossible.   As Peter Ackroyd
has noted, apparent differences between the Books of Chronicles
and Ezra-Nehemiah may be due to differences in the sources and in
the Chronicler's use of them.[60]

Finally, even the successful rebuttal of one of the arguments
for common authorship is an inadequate basis for the abandonment
of a consensus that adduces a variety of additional arguments in
support of its thesis.   To be successful a new theory of the
authorship or editorial history of Chronicles, Ezra and Nehemiah
will have to dispose of all the major arguments in support of
common authorship and propose a more probable interpretation of
the evidence at hand.   The latter remains to be done, but the former
is attempted by H.G.M. Williamson, who devotes fully half of his
monograph on the Chronicler's view of Israel to a comprehensive
and sustained disputation of the prevailing view that Ezra-Nehemiah
was an original part of the Chronicler's Work.[61]

Williamson begins by noting the fact that Zunz's arguments
for a history work comprised of Chronicles, Ezra and Nehemiah
with subsequent refinements "convinces the overwhelming majority
of scholars."[62]   These arguments, Williamson finds, are in the main
the four following:

1.   The presence of the opening sentences of Ezra at the end
     of 2 Chronicles.
2.   The evidence of 1 Esdras, which starts at 2 Chron. 35
     and continues without interruption into Ezra.
3.   The similarity between the books in style and choice of
     vocabulary.
4.   The similarity of outlook, interests and theology.[63]

---

[59] F.M. Cross, "The History of the Biblical Text in the Light of Discoveries in
the Judaean Desert," in F.M. Cross and S. Talmon (eds.), *Qumran and the
History of the Biblical Text* (Cambridge, 1975), pp. 188-93 [= *HTR*, LVII
(1964), 281-99]; cf. n. 5 above.

[60] Ackroyd, *1 and 2 Chronicles, Ezra, Nehemiah*, pp. 22-23.

[61] Williamson, *Israel*, pp. 5-82.

[62] Williamson, *Israel*, p. 5.

[63] Williamson, *Israel*, pp. 5-6.

While it is clearly his conviction that the Chronicler authored essentially our present Books of Chronicles (no more and very little less), Williamson does not provide an argument for that theory. His method is rather to take up one by one the four major arguments for including Ezra-Nehemiah in the Chronicler's Work and attempt to neutralize them by pointing out their weaknesses. His thesis, then, is simply that the arguments for common authorship of the Books of Chronicles and Ezra-Nehemiah are inconclusive. His conclusion is that since they are now separate and there are no compelling arguments that they were ever otherwise, they should be regarded as independent works and investigated as such.[64]

Williamson's work is a major contribution to the question of the extent of the Chronicler's Work; if it does not lead to a new consensus, it has at least stated the question. Further investigation of the extent of the Chronicler's Work, including the present one, must come to terms with both Williamson's arguments and his conclusion.

2 Chronicles 36:22-23 and Ezra 1:1-3a

Williamson begins his argument with what he regards as the most important piece of evidence in favor of common authorship, namely the near identity of the end of 2 Chronicles and the beginning of Ezra (i.e., 2 Chron. 36:22-23 = Ezra 1:1-3a). The standard explanation for this overlap is that it was intended to identify the original connection between Chronicles and Ezra-Nehemiah.[65] The reason for ever separating the two was then explained as a consequence of the history of the formation of the Canon, in which Ezra-Nehemiah by virtue of the fact that it continued the already canonical Deuteronomistic History gained a place before Chronicles, which was merely a parallel history.[66]

Williamson objects to this interpretation on both internal and external grounds. First, he cites Welch's view that the overlap in fact indicates the opposite of common authorship because "men do not take the trouble to stitch together two documents, unless they

---

[64] Williamson, *Israel*, p. 70.

[65] Williamson, *Israel*, p. 7.

[66] Williamson, *Israel*, p. 7. Williamson quotes E. Curtis and A. Madsen, *A Critical and Exegetical Commentary on the Books of Chronicles* (New York, 1910), p. 3, as a typical representative of this view.

have been originally separate."[67]   The logic here is obscure; while the fact of the "stitching together" evidences an immediately preceding status as separate documents, it can shed no clear light on the original status of the work. The evidence (i.e., the overlap) could indicate an intention to rejoin two separated entities which in their original state were a unity, or it could, as Welch views it, indicate that independent documents were joined together. The simple fact of the overlap is incapable of discriminating between these options. Though Williamson does not note it, that in itself is sufficient proof that the argument for common authorship based on this evidence is inconclusive.

The fact that 2 Chron. 36:22-23 appears to be derived from Ezra 1:1, which Williamson has correctly noted,[68] does not argue against common authorship.   Rather, those who regard the separation of Chronicles and Ezra-Nehemiah as secondary regard the repetition of the beginning of Ezra at the end of 2 Chronicles as secondary too, and cite 1 Esdras, which picks up the history at 2 Chron. 35 and continues into Ezra without the overlap, as evidence.[69]   The ending of 2 Chronicles, derived from Cyrus' decree in Ezra 1:1-3, provides a link to the book of Ezra-Nehemiah and a positive, or optimistic, ending for the Book of Chronicles. Like Kings, Chronicles does not end with the conquest of Jerusalem, but with an indication that history is finally moving in favor of the Israelites.[70]

On external grounds, Williamson's critique is that there is no evidence to support the view that Chronicles and Ezra-Nehemiah were separated in the process of their canonization. In this regard, Williamson follows Willi, who pointed out that there is no evidence that the canonicity of Chronicles was ever disputed or that it was canonized subsequent to Ezra-Nehemiah.[71]   The problem is that there is precious little evidence of how or when either Chronicles or Ezra-Nehemiah was canonized.   The theory that a separation

---

[67] A.C. Welch, *Post-Exilic Judaism* (Edinburgh and London, 1935), p. 186, quoted in Williamson, *Israel*, p. 7.

[68] Williamson, *Israel*, p. 9.

[69] Cf. e.g., Cross, "A Reconstruction," p. 8.

[70] Eissfeldt, *The Old Testament*, p. 531.

[71] T. Willi, *Die Chronik als Auslegung; Untersuchen zur literarischen Gestaltung der historischen Überlieferung Israels* (Göttingen, 1972), pp. 176-84. Cf. Williamson, *Israel*, pp. 10-11.

occurred in the process of the redaction and canonization of the Chronicler's Work is an attempt to explain the overlap at the end of Chronicles and the beginning of Ezra. Williamson shows that the theory cannot be proved. We knew that.[72] The burden on Williamson is to provide a better (provable seems to be his requirement) explanation for the overlap; this he has not done.

On the other hand, Williamson has made clear that the repetition of Ezra 1:1-3a at 2 Chron. 36:22-23 does not require the theory of common authorship. He overlooks the fact that it does constitute a joining of Chronicles with Ezra-Nehemiah at least editorially if not originally. Which is to say that, whether originally or only secondarily, we must deal with a history work comprised of Chronicles, Ezra and Nehemiah.

<u>The Evidence of the Greek Versions</u>

1 Esdras corresponds with parts of the Hebrew 2 Chronicles, Ezra and Nehemiah. It begins with 2 Chron. 35:1 and continues, without interruption or repetition, with the Ezra narrative including Neh. 8. Since Zunz that fact has been cited as evidence of an earlier (or original) version of the Chronicler's Work. This theory would maintain that 1 Esdras was a translation of the Chronicler's Work which was completed before Ezra-Nehemiah was separated from 1 and 2 Chronicles.[73] Because Pohlmann[74] argues just that position, Williamson's method in this section of his book is to follow Pohlmann step by step and demonstrate what he takes to be the weakness of his case.

To begin with, Williamson concurs (without discussion) with Pohlmann that 1 Esdras "Does give us a translation of our MT."[75]

---

[72] As Williamson himself pointed out, Eissfeldt, who supports the theory, recognizes that it is not proved. Cf. Eissfeldt, *The Old Testament*, p. 567, and Williamson, *Israel*, p. 10.

[73] Cf. Batten, *The Books of Ezra and Nehemiah*, p. 2; H. Howorth, "The Real Character and the Importance of the First Book of Esdras, II," *The Academy*, XLIII (1893), p. 60, and recently Cross, "A Reconstruction," pp. 7-8.

[74] K-F. Pohlmann, *Studien sum Dritten Esra. Ein Beitrag zur Frage nach dem Ursprünglich Schluss des Chronistischen Geschichtswerks* (Göttingen, 1970).

[75] Williamson, *Israel*, p. 13. This wording is important. Williamson does not say that 1 Esdras is a translation of MT because he believes that the author of 1 Esdras reorganized his MT *Vorlage*. It is thus a compilation of MT Ezra-Nehemiah, not a translation (see below).

This is an important conclusion, but it is not universally affirmed.[76] If 1 Esdras is based on a non-Masoretic Hebrew recension, then the problem of its relationship to MT Ezra-Nehemiah is complicated. Also, Williamson and Pohlmann are agreed that the ending of the Chronicler's Work must be determined on the basis of internal considerations alone. Thus as Williamson puts it,

> If on internal grounds...we are satisfied that 1 Chronicles-Ezra. 10/Neh. 8 is an original and unified composition, then 1 Esdras could be adduced as valuable supporting evidence. If, on the other hand, it was decided that 2 Chron. 36 furnished the original conclusion of the Chronicler's Work, 1 Esdras could not by itself overthrow that decision. It would be necessary only to postulate additions to the Chronicler's Work before the translation of 1 Esdras.[77]

Williamson's conviction is that the Chronicler's Work does indeed end with 2 Chron. 36, and thus he regards the second position as possible. Since it is in part drawn from silence, he prefers to argue that 1 Esdras is in fact not a translation of an earlier version of the Chronicler's Work, but is rather a compilation (based on the MT of Ezra-Nehemiah) which seeks to resolve the literary and historical problems of the relationship of Ezra and Nehemiah.

Williamson must first dispose of Pohlmann's unfounded stipulation that 1 Esdras is a fragment of a translation that originally included all of 1 and 2 Chronicles[78] It seems certain from the beginning of 1 Esdras that the original opening has been damaged. Williamson, however, argues that "not so very much has been lost."[79] This conclusion is based on two verses (1 Esdras 1:21-22, Ev. 1:23-24) which are lacking in the MT. Against Walde, Williamson argues that they are original to 1 Esdras, and are a clue to its original beginning.[80] Williamson's reasoning is as follows:[81]

---

[76] E.g., Cross, "A Reconstruction," p. 8.

[77] Williamson, *Israel*, p. 13.

[78] Williamson, *Israel*, pp. 14-15. Cf. Pohlmann, *Dritten Esra*, pp. 32-33.

[79] Williamson, *Israel*, p. 20.

[80] Williamson, *Israel*, pp. 16-18. Against C.C. Torrey, Williamson argues that 1 Esd. 1:21-22 was never part of MT. Cf. Williamson, *Israel*, p. 17 and n. 1.

[81] See Williamson, *Israel*, pp. 18-21.

1. The Deuteronomist's explanation of the exile is that guilt accumulated to the point that not even Josiah's righteousness could forestall the judgment pronounced against Manasseh (2 Kgs. 21:10-12). Josiah's untimely death is in that context passed off as the reward for his piety. He will not have to see the judgment that is about to fall (2 Kgs. 22:20).

2. By contrast, in Chronicles retribution is immediate. Manasseh himself was exiled for his sin (2 Chron. 33:11), and the exile of Judah was the result of the sins of Zedekiah and his contemporaries (2 Chron. 36:12-17). The death of Josiah is the immediate consequence of his disobedience in engaging Neco (2 Chron. 25:20-23).

3. In 1 Esdras 1:21-22 we have a different explanation for the exile. Notwithstanding the piety of Josiah, the sins of his subjects were sufficient to bring about the exile. The language by which these sins are described is reminiscent of the condemnation of Manasseh's reign (in both 2 Kgs. 21:9 and 2 Chron. 33:9).

4. From this Williamson draws two conclusions. First, the telescoping of events from Manasseh's reign to that of Josiah suggests that 1 Esdras had not already described the period of Manasseh, but that its account began later, perhaps with the accession of Josiah. And secondly, that the different interpretation of the exile reinforces the conclusion that 1 Esdras is independent from the Chronicler's Work. It follows, of course, that Ezra-Nehemiah is independent from Chronicles as well. "This leaves (Chronicles)," Williamson concludes, "as the unique witness of its particular interpretation of the exile..."[82] namely, as the immediate consequence of the sins of Zedekiah and the people of his day.

Neither of these conclusions is tenable. The latter completely overlooks 1 Esdras 1:45-51 which like 2 Chron. 36:12-17 (and, indeed, based on it) states that the exile is the direct consequence of the sins of Zedekiah. Williamson's silence at this point is surprising, especially since the authenticity of this passage, unlike 1 Esdras 1:21-22, is unchallenged. As for his first conclusion, it is a rather large jump from the verbal similarity of 1 Esdras 1:22 to 2

---

[82] Williamson, *Israel*, p. 20.

Kgs. 21:9 and 2 Chron. 33:9 to the interpretation that 1 Esdras has attributed events of Manasseh's time to that of Josiah. Several more likely possibilities lie closer to hand. Thus it may be that the verbal similarity is like the evaluations of the monarchs, that is, formulaic. Or, in light of 1 Esdras 1:45-51, 1 Esdras 1:21-22 may indeed be a gloss on 1 Esdras, as Walde argued.[83] In the final analysis all that can be said about the original beginning of 1 Esdras is that it is not extant. The evidence simply does not warrant Pohlmann's assertion or Williamson's "guess."[84]

As to the ending of 1 Esdras, Williamson again concurs with Pohlmann that it too is fragmentary. Pohlmann, however, argues that the lost conclusion of 1 Esdras can be reconstructed on the basis of Josephus' use of it for his *Antiquities*. In this Williamson disagrees.

For his presentation of the chapters of Ezra and Nehemiah in *Antiquities* XI, 1-183, Josephus utilized 1 Esdras (for Ezra, XI, 1-158) and Neh. 1:1-7:4 (for Nehemiah, XI, 159-183). This suggests to Pohlmann that Josephus did not know the canonical books in which Neh. 8 follows Neh. 7 and not Ezra 10 (as it does in 1 Esdras and *Antiquities*). Williamson counters this in two ways. First, it is the use of 1 Esdras, which puts Neh. 8 after Ezra 10, that accounts for the order of Josephus' account and requires that he treat Nehemiah separately. But more important is Williamson's contention that 1 Esdras 9:37 proves that the *Vorlage* of 1 Esdras had Neh. 8 after Neh. 7 and not Ezra 10. Pohlmann himself acknowledges that this verse poses the most difficult challenge to his position.[85] It is therefore necessary for us to consider it in some detail.

The relevant texts are 1 Esdras 9:37-39 and Nehemiah 7:72-8:1 (Ev. 7:73-8:1), as follows:

1 Esdras 9:37-39
The priests and the Levites and the men of Israel settled in Jerusalem and in the country. On the new moon of the seventh month, when the sons of Israel were in their settlements, (v. 38) the whole multitude gathered with one accord into the open square before the east gate of the temple; (v. 39) and they told Ezra the chief priest and

[83] B. Walde, *Die Esdrasbücher der Septuaginta* (Freiburg, 1913), pp. 88-90.
[84] Williamson, *Israel*, p. 20.
[85] Pohlmann, *Dritten Esra*, p. 66.

reader to bring the law of Moses which had been given
by the Lord God of Israel.

Nehemiah 7:72-8:1
So the priests, the Levites, the gatekeepers, the singers,
some of the people, the temple servants, and all Israel,
lived in their towns. And when the seventh month had
come, the children of Israel were in their towns. (8:1)
And all the people gathered as one man into the square
before the Water Gate; and they told Ezra the scribe to
bring the book of the law of Moses which the Lord had
given to Israel.

What is at stake, we may recall, is the status of 1 Esdras.
Does it, as most scholars assume, represent an earlier version of
Ezra and Nehemiah, or is it a secondary compilation based on the
canonical books? If 1 Esdras 9:37 is a translation of Neh. 7:72 (Ev.
7:73), as Williamson affirms, then it is clear that the compiler of 1
Esdras knew the material as it is presently arranged, that is, with
Neh. 8 following Neh. 7. At first glance this seems to be the case.
1 Esdras 9:1-36 takes up the narrative from Ezra 10:6 and follows it
apparently through verse 44. 1 Esdras 9:37-55 follows and seems
to be based on Neh. 7:72-8:12.[86] Moreover, Williamson points out
that a comparison of Neh. 7:70-8:1 with Ezra 2:68-3:1 suggests that
the time reference (ויגע החדש השביעי) belonged originally to what
precedes and not to what follows.[87] Since 1 Esdras 9:37 appears to
translate this reference 1 Esdras, he concludes, must have been
compiled after Neh. 8 had been joined to Neh. 7. Williamson's
statement to this effect is somewhat cryptic, and it will be helpful to
rehearse the evidence on which it is based.
     The problem of the relationship of 1 Esdras 9:37 to Neh.
7:72b is complicated by the fact that the same verse occurs at Ezra
3:1 (= 1 Esdras 5:46). The following schematic arrangements will
clarify these relationships.

---

[86] And a phrase from 8:13?
[87] Williamson, *Israel*, p. 32.

1.   1 Esdras 5:7-70

		1 Esdras	Ezra	Nehemiah
a.	Census	5:7-45	2:1-70	7:6-72a
b.	Time Reference	5:46	3:1	7:72b
c.	Joshua/Altar/ Sukkoth	5:47-70	3:1-13	

We note that:
1)   Ezra 2:1-3:1 (which includes the time reference) is repeated at Neh. 7:6-72b. What follows in Neh. 8 is not equal to what follows in Ezra 3. This suggests that the date goes with the preceding material.
2)   1 Esdras follows Ezra's order.

2.   1 Esdras 8:88-9:55

		1 Esdras	Ezra	Nehemiah
a.	Divorce	8:88-9:36	10:1-44	
b.	Time Reference	9:37[88]		7:72b
c.	Ezra/Law	9:38-55		8:1-2(13)

We note that:
1)   1 Esdras 8:88-9:55 follows Ezra 10 to its end and then takes up the Ezra material of Neh. 8 beginning with 7:72b.
2)   This suggests that in the *Vorlage* of 1 Esdras Neh. 8 followed Neh. 7 and not Ezra 10.
3)   The compiler of 1 Esdras knows the time reference in both the context of Ezra 2/3 and Neh. 7/8, but unlike Ezra-Nehemiah he does not repeat the census list (Ezra 2 = Neh. 7). 1 Esdras, thus, is in some sense a compilation.

The clear implication, then, of this evidence is that the *Vorlage* of 1 Esdras, like the MT, had Neh. 8 after Neh. 7 and not after Ezra 10. It follows that 1 Esdras, in rearranging the material, is a compilation, and can shed no light on earlier editions of Chronicles and Ezra-Nehemiah. To hold otherwise one must argue that 9:37 is

---

[88] 1 Esdras 9:37 does not translate Neh. 7:72b exactly, but cf. Williamson, *Israel*, p. 35.

a gloss to 1 Esdras, as Mowinckel does,[89] or that in spite of appearances 9:37 is in fact not a translation of Neh. 7:72b, as Pohlmann maintains.[90] As Williamson noted, the decisive point in favor of either of these views is the theory of the common authorship of Chronicles, Ezra and Nehemiah.[91] Apart from this circular argument neither view can claim the support which would be necessary to overthrow the obvious conclusion that 1 Esdras 9:37 is based on Neh. 7:72b.

In sum, we must disagree with both Pohlmann and Williamson on the problem of the beginning of 1 Esdras. All that can reasonably be argued is that the original beginning is no longer extant. On the other hand, Williamson is certainly correct in rejecting Pohlmann's claim that the original ending of 1 Esdras can be reconstructed from *The Antiquities* of Josephus. The ending, too, is simply lost. Thus we are not in a position to speculate on the original extent of 1 Esdras. It is a fragment of a larger work.

What is crucial to our investigation, however, is the question of its *Vorlage*. As we have seen, a straightforward examination of 1 Esdras 9:37 leads us to conclude that the compiler of 1 Esdras knew the canonical arrangement of the material. From that it follows that 1 Esdras provides no evidence for earlier versions of the Chronicler's Work.

The Similarity of Vocabulary and Style in Chronicles, Ezra and Nehemiah

On pages 37-59 Williamson deals with the widely-held view that Chronicles and Ezra-Nehemiah evidence a similarity in vocabulary and style that is so remarkable as to require the hypothesis of common authorship. His procedure is to evaluate the items on Driver's[92] and Curtis-Madsen's[93] lists on the basis of a carefully constructed set of criteria[94] to determine the extent to

---

[89] S. Mowinckel, *Studien zu dem Buche Ezra-Nehemia I: Die nachchronistische Redaction des Buches. Die Listen.* (Oslo, 1964), pp. 21-25.

[90] Pohlmann, *Dritten Esra*, pp. 68-71.

[91] Williamson, *Israel*, p. 34.

[92] S.R. Driver, *An Introduction to the Literature of the Old Testament* (Gloucester, 1972), pp. 535-39.

[93] Curtis and Madsen, *Chronicles*, pp. 28-36.

[94] Williamson, *Israel*, pp. 39-40.

which Chronicles and Ezra-Nehemiah do in fact share stylistic peculiarities. His contribution in this regard is important because, as he points out,[95] the lists were not intended to demonstrate common authorship, but are widely and uncritically put to that task; his is the first serious attempt to determine the extent to which the lists do support common authorship.

Williamson's presentation of the evidence is thorough and very accurate;[96] his conclusions, however, are heavily influenced by dubious methodological presuppositions. It is entirely to his credit that he states his criteria clearly and at the outset. Yet one would not expect that much evidence could be found in a unified work that would satisfy them. Thus, for example, it is not at all clear that common authorship of 1 and 2 Chronicles could be demonstrated on the basis of his criteria for the simple reason that very few words appear only in 1 and 2 Chronicles, distributed equally between them, and for which other words are used elsewhere.[97]

Even with so rigorous a method, Williamson finds latitude to interpret the evidence in such a way that his conclusion of separate authorship is supported. Thus if a word meets all his criteria for proving common authorship, it can still be explained as an indication of common interest rather than common authorship.[98] On the other hand, a word which appears to be a part of the vocabulary of late biblical Hebrew and occurs in both Chronicles and Ezra-Nehemiah can be taken either as evidence of separate authorship or disregarded as the common language of the period.[99]

---

[95] Williamson, *Israel*, pp. 37-38.

[96] With, to my knowledge, one exception. Williamson on p. 59 (following Curtis-Madsen p. 33) states that שמחה גדלה occurs "twice in Chr., three times in Ezr. and twice in Neh." I find the phrase four times in Chronicles, never in Ezra and three times in Nehemiah, i.e., 1 Chron. 29:9, 22; 2 Chron. 30:21, 26; Neh. 8:12, 17; 12:43.

[97] As his criteria would require. It appears that six of Driver's forty-six items (i.e., numbers 10, 13, 22, 31, 36, 42) are suggestive of common authorship of 1 and 2 Chronicles.

[98] E.g., החיחש pp. 45-46, נקבו בשמות p. 47, משׁורר and שׁוערים p. 51, הלל (ל)יהוה and הלל abs. p. 51.

[99] Cp. e.g., דרש p. 54 with נשׂא p. 52.

Finally, due weight must be given to the fact that several items in Williamson's list do tend to support his view that Chronicles and Ezra-Nehemiah had separate authors.[100]

Williamson's study has not proved that Chronicles and Ezra-Nehemiah had different authors; it has shown that the lists of Driver and Curtis-Madsen do not *prove* unity of authorship. In light of the methodological problems and the fact that so little of the literature of the period is extant, one can hardly avoid skepticism about the whole enterprise.

Interests, Outlook and Theology

The fourth and last argument in favor of the theory of common authorship of Chronicles and Ezra-Nehemiah, which Williamson attempts to discredit is the ubiquitous, although varying in its details, contention that the books exhibit the same interests, outlook, and theology. To be credible such a claim must be based on careful evaluation of specific similarities, but in fact is usually asserted in generalities. Williamson is of course arguing the opposite point of view and so is of the persuasion that differences in outlook are more significant than similarities. His treatment of this topic deals, then, with five main discontinuities between the books of Chronicles and Ezra-Nehemiah and closes with an assortment of minor differences and the conclusion that, while the two have some interests in common, the treatment of these interests and the other points of contrast strongly suggest separate authors.

Williamson's argument in this regard suffers, however, from inadequate attention to the relationship of our Chronicles and Ezra-Nehemiah to their sources. Thus in his treatment of mixed marriages he contrasts the omission in Chronicles of 1 Kgs. 11:1-3 (Solomon's mixed marriages) with Neh. 13:26 which refers to them.[101] Williamson's view is that one author would not have missed "such a golden opportunity"[102] to make his point. The flaw in this comparison is that Williamson has already assigned Neh. 13:26 to the Nehemiah Memoir which was incorporated virtually without alteration into Nehemiah.[103] Likewise, one wonders

---

[100] Especially nos. 5, 7, 17, and 18 (Williamson, *Israel*, pp. 54-56).

[101] Williamson, *Israel*, pp. 60-61.

[102] Williamson, *Israel*, p. 61.

[103] Williamson, *Israel*, p. 41 nn. 1, 2.

whether the difference in the use of covenant traditions reflects different authors or different sources. Certainly the emphasis in Chronicles on the Davidic covenant is a reflection of its deuteronomistic source.

On the other hand, Williamson's comments on the treatment of the fall of the Northern Kingdom and the theory of immediate retribution are more persuasive.[104] The second half of his book, moreover, makes a compelling case for his view that Israel in Chronicles is not the remnant that is so identified in Ezra-Nehemiah. These points could, perhaps be challenged on the basis of disparate sources, but the question would then arise as to why such different viewpoints would be joined, without harmonization, into a single unified history work.

Williamson's intention in this section of his book is not to prove separate authorship of Chronicles and Ezra-Nehemiah, but merely to show that the claim of common authorship, to the extent that it is based on similarity of ideology, is unsubstantiated and, indeed, overlooks significant contrasts between the books. With this we concur.

Summary and Conclusion

In the last two decades the widely-held hypothesis of common authorship of the Books of Chronicles and Ezra-Nehemiah has suffered both a frontal and a flank assault. The critique by Freedman which was taken up and greatly advanced by Cross was mainly a proposal for a new understanding of the editorial history of the books in question, and thus attacked the Zunz hypothesis indirectly, even if necessarily. The work of Japhet and now Williamson, however, challenges the hypothesis directly, but unlike Freeman, and especially Cross, provides no systematic new interpretation of the evidence at hand. Williamson has, however, brought to light basic weaknesses in the Freedman-Cross reconstruction.[105]

Williamson has shown that the duplication of Ezra 1:1-3a at 2 Chron. 36:22-23, could be used as evidence of separate authorship as well as of common authorship. In his treatment of 1 Esdras 9:37,

---

[104] Williamson, *Israel*, pp. 66-68.

[105] Primarily their over-evaluation of the significance of the overlap at the end of Chronicles and beginning of Ezra, and the assumption that 1 Esdras is a translation of an earlier version of the Chronicler's History Work.

he has provided a strong argument against the view that 1 Esdras represents an early (or original) version of the Chronicler's Work; he has also provided a plausible explanation of Josephus' treatment of his sources for Ezra and Nehemiah. The treatment of ideology, vocabulary and style is less conclusive, but differences between Chronlicles and Ezra-Nehemiah are identified and do weaken the theory of common authorship. At the present state of our knowledge and in light of the slender and ambiguous evidence at our disposal, we can only agree with Williamson's conclusion that the theory that one author composed or compiled an original history comprising Chronicles, Ezra and Nehemiah is unproved.

That fact constitutes for Williamson the warrant for his view of independent authorship of the books, and is the grounds on which he can exclude Ezra-Nehemiah from his investigation of Israel in the Chronicler's Work. Because Ezra-Nehemiah presents a view of Israel which conflicts with the view Williamson discovers in Chronicles, his thesis requires that they have different authors. For that reason Williamson is satisfied to argue that such evidence for common authorship as we have fails to prove the thesis, and does not feel constrained, having demonstrated that, to provide a better interpretation of the data. Thus, while common authorship of the books must be regarded as unproved, Williamson's theory of separate authors likewise remains to be demonstrated.

The present investigation of claims to authority in Chronicles, Ezra and Nehemiah is not the place to resolve this stalemate. Indeed, the emphasis on the original extent of such a source-based work as the Chronicler's History seems misplaced. Moreover, as Ackroyd reminds us, every copy of an ancient text was in a sense a new edition in which changes, intentional and otherwise, were made.[106] The books of Chronicles, Ezra and Nehemiah appear to have been particularly vulnerable to such editorial activity, perhaps, although it is really only a guess, owing to its lack of canonicity.[107] A full description of the editorial history of the Chronicler's Work remains, therefore, as a major task requiring, and perhaps deserving, an extended treatment. I am not optimistic, however, that the evidence would yield a theory that was at once specific and capable of commanding widespread assent. At present scholars agree in general that our books of Chronicles, Ezra and Nehemiah are not as they left the original writer, but there is very little

---

[106] Ackroyd, *1 and 2 Chronicles, Ezra, Nehemiah*, p. 23.
[107] Ackroyd, *1 and 2 Chronicles, Ezra, Nehemiah*, p. 23.

agreement when it comes to specifying exactly how they differ from the original. Thus in the last two decades we have seen four major attempts to discover the extent of the original; these have produced four different theories. Kellermann (1967) argued that the Chronicler's Work originally included most of the present Chronicles, Ezra and Nehemiah (although there was a post-Chronistic redaction), including even the present arrangement of the Ezra and Nehemiah traditions.[108] Pohlmann (1970), on the other hand, argued on the basis of the material in 3 Ezra (1 Esdras) that the entirety of the Nehemiah material was secondary to the original work.[109] The History, he claimed, originally ended with the reading of the law and celebration of Sukkoth in Neh. 8, which immediately followed the account in Ezra 10 of the purification of the community by divorcing foreign wives.[110] Cross' contribution to this issue (1975), which is discussed at some length above, is both more ambitious and briefer than that of Pohlmann and Kellermann, neither of which rates even a footnote.[111] This is all the more surprising since Cross' Chr 2 corresponds with Pohlmann's view of the original Chronicler's Work, and is likewise based on the evidence of 1 Esdras.[112] For the original edition of the work, however, Cross depends on Freedman, who argued that it included only 1 Chron. 10 - 2 Chron. 34 plus the *Vorlage* of 1 Edras 1:1-5:65 (= 2 Chron. 34:1 - Ezra 3:13).[113] Williamson (1977), as we have seen, rejected all of these positions in favor of the view that the Chronicler's History originally contained virtually all of 1 and 2 Chronicles (including 1 Chron. 1-9) but none of Ezra and Nehemiah.[114]

Resolving the issues that divide these scholars (assuming, for the moment, that to be possible) would be a major undertaking and

---

[108] Ulrich Kellermann, *Nehemia: Quellen, Überlieferung und Geschichte,* BZAW, CII (Berlin, 1967).

[109] K-F. Pohlmann, *Studien sum Dritten Esra. Ein Beitrag zur Frage nach dem Ursprünglich Schluss des Chronistischen Geschichtswerks* (Göttingen, 1970).

[110] Pohlmann, *Dritten Esra*, pp. 143-45.

[111] Frank Moore Cross, "A Reconstruction of the Judean Restoration," *JBL*, XCIV (1975), 4-18.

[112] Cross, "A Reconstruction," pp. 7-9, 11.

[113] Cross, "A Reconstruction," pp. 12-13. Cf. Freedman, "Purpose," pp. 436-42.

[114] Williamson, *Israel*, pp. 5-82.

is beyond the scope of the present work. It is imperative, nevertheless, to describe the position assumed in what follows even if the reader is only referred to others for the full argumentation on the basis of which this position is taken.

By the Chronicler's History Work I mean the books of Chronicles, Ezra and Nehemiah. The title is misleading, however, in that, like calling the Pentateuch the Book of Moses, it implies, especially to us moderns, that the completed work was the creative product of a single writer. That such was not the case for the Chronicler's History is no more certain than for the Pentateuch. Both include a number of sources and are the products of complex redactional histories during which these sources were edited and combined, copied and rewritten. The specific stages in the process by which the Chronicler's Work was formed were numerous, and are, I believe, for the most part unrecoverable. I have some confidence, however, that a major penultimate stage or edition can be identified. And while it is clearly not the case that one author composed all the material of which this edition is comprised, the structure of the work supports the thesis that its compiler viewed it as a finished product, and it is indeed very close to what some regard as the original Chronicler's Work. This penultimate, if not original, edition included (excepting numerous short glosses) all of the books of Chronicles, Ezra and Nehemiah except for the Nehemiah material (i.e. Neh. 1:1-7:5a; 11:1-2; 12:27-43; 13:4-14).

There are three main objections to the identification of such an edition. First, it is commonly assumed that 1 Chron. 1-9 is (in whole or in part) a late addition.[115] Second, it has been argued that the Ezra narrative had a different author/compiler than that of the books of Chronicles.[116] And third, some argue that most of the Nehemiah material was included in the original edition.[117]

I include 1 Chron. 1-9 on the basis of arguments advanced by Williamson that the chapters are essentially a unity with "a considerable number of points of contact...with the (subsequent)

---

[115] Welch, *Judaism*, pp. 186-87, and Cross, "A Reconstruction," pp. 12-13, regard the whole of Chron. 1-9 as late. Wilhelm Rudolph, *Chronikbücher*, Handbuch zum Alten Testament, 21/1 (Tübingen, 1955), pp. 1-93, argued that much of the genealogical material was late. Ackroyd, *1 and 2 Chronicles, Ezra, Nehemiah*, pp. 23, 30, assumes some expansions of these chapters.

[116] This is the position of Japhet and Williamson, cf. above.

[117] This is Kellermann's view.

narrative."[118]   In addition to such points of contact as the emphasis on David, immediate retribution, and the neglect of Moses and the exodus, Williamson cites stylistic features common only to the genealogies and the rest of Chronicles, such as the interest in the role of Jacob (who is called Israel twelve times by the Chronicler), in the history of Israel, and in the Chronistic style of the account of the battle in 1 Chron. 5:20.[119]   In my view these points do not constitute proof that the chapters were originally part of the History, but in the absence of any good reason to exclude 1 Chron. 1-9, they will suffice.

Contrary to Williamson, however, I find the evidence that the Ezra material was written by the compiler of the books of Chronicles to be persuasive. This view has been presented at length by Torrey, more recently by Kellermann, and is accepted by many others.[120] Finally, I have accepted Pohlmann's thesis that the Chronicler's History circulated independently of the Nehemiah traditions for several reasons. While I have some reservations as to whether 1 Esdras is in fact a translation of this edition (the original edition, he believes) of the Chronicler's Work, especially in light of the apparent fact that 1 Esdras 9:37 translates Neh. 7:72,[121] his argument from the overall structure of the work is compelling,[122] and it is clear from other texts that the Ezra and Nehemiah traditions were preserved independently.[123]   The investigation of references to the law in the Chronicler's History which follows, therefore, takes the whole of Chronicles, Ezra and Nehemiah as its subject, but the Nehemiah Memoir will be treated separately, on the assumption that it was an addition to a well-structured work.

---

[118] Williamson, *1 and 2 Chronicles*, p. 39.

[119] Williamson, *1 and 2 Chronicles*, pp. 39, 65. Cf. Williamson, *Israel*, pp. 71-82; and M.D. Johnson, *The Purpose of the Biblical Genealogies*, Society for New Testament Studies. Monograph Series VIII (Cambridge, 1969), pp. 44-55.

[120] Torrey, *Ezra Studies*, pp. 223-25, 238-48; Kellermann, *Nehemia*, pp. 56-69.

[121] Cf. above pp. 60-63.

[122] Pohlmann, *Dritten Esra*, pp. 143-48. Cf. the discussion in Ralph W. Klein, "Ezra and Nehemiah in Recent Studies," *Magnalia Dei, the mighty acts of God*, eds. F.M. Cross, et al., (Garden City, 1976), pp. 36869.

[123] 2 Macc. 1 and Ecclesiasticus (ben Sira) 49 preserve Nehemiah traditions in contexts where one is surprised to find no mention of Ezra. 1 and 2 Esdras, on the other hand, have much to tell about Ezra, but do not refer to Nehemiah. Cf. Ackroyd, *1 and 2 Chronicles, Ezra, Nehemiah*, p. 25.

The Date of the Chronicler's History Work

The view of Torrey[124] and Noth,[125] that the Chronicler is to be dated in the Greek Period ca. 250 B.C.E., must be abandoned, as Albright has shown.[126] It is still the case, however, that a late date in the Persian Period, about the middle of the fourth century, best satisfies the limited evidence at hand.[127] This evidence includes the following points:

1)   The genealogy of the Davidic family in 1 Chron. 3:17-24, although somewhat problematic, seems to give six generations following Zerubbabel which brings us down to the beginning of the fourth century.[128]

2)   The list of post-exilic high priests, Neh. 12:10-11, 22, brings us to the same period.[129] The last high priest seems to be Johanan (Ezra 10:6), who was high priest in 411 B.C.E.[130] Neh. 12:11, 22 names his son and successor, who nowhere is identified as high priest.[131]

---

[124] Torrey, *Ezra Studies*, pp. 30, 35.

[125] M. Noth, *Überlieferungsgeschichtliche Studien I*, pp. 150-55.

[126] Albright, "Personality," pp. 107-19. Albright's arguments were decisive for most scholars. An exception is R. Pfeiffer, *Introduction*, pp. 811-12, and "Chronicles, 1 and 2," *Interpreter's Dictionary of the Bible*, Vol. 1 (Nashville and New York, 1962), p. 581.

[127] This is a widely-shared view. Cf. Ackroyd, *1 and 2 Chronicles, Ezra, Nehemiah*, pp. 25-26; Eissfeldt, *The Old Testament*, p. 540; Williamson, *1 and 2 Chronicles*, pp. 15-16. A number of scholars, however, date the work slightly earlier in the first half of the fourth century. Cf. Albright, "Personality," p. 119; Rudolph, *Esra und Nehemia*, pp. XXIV-XXV; Myers, *I Chronicles*, p. LXXXVII; even Cross, "A Reconstruction," p. 12, dates the final version, Chr 3, ca. 400 or a bit later.

[128] Albright, "Personality," pp. 108-12; Williamson, *Israel*, p. 83; Myers, *I Chronicles*, p. LXXXIX; Rudolph, *Chronikbücher*, p. X, and *Esra und Nehemia*, p. XXV; Curtis and Madsen, *Chronicles*, pp. 5-6.

[129] Albright, "Personality," pp. 112-13.

[130] Myers, *Ezra. Nehemiah*, pp. LXVIII-LXIX. Cf. *AP* 30.

[131] Myers, *Ezra. Nehemiah*, pp. LXVIII-LXIX.

3)   The last king mentioned is Artaxerxes II (405-359); Ezra 7:1, 7, 11, 12, 21; 8:1.[132]

4)   If it is true that the Chronicler's Work circulated at first independently of the Nehemiah traditions, then the last events recorded by the Chronicler are connected with Ezra's mission. Since we have adopted the view first argued by van Hoonacker that dates Ezra's commission (Ezra 7) to the seventh year of Artaxerxes II, that is 398 B.C.E.,[133] we have a *terminus a quo* early in the fourth century; the *terminus ad quem* suggested by the absence of Hellenistic influence is the end of the Persian period.

---

[132] Unless the references are to Artaxerxes I (465-425), in which case Darius II (424-405) would be the last. Cf. Myers, *Ezra. Nehemiah*, p. LXIX.

[133] Cf. Rowley, "Chronological Order," pp. 137-68, and Kellermann, "Esradatierung," pp. 55-87, for a full discussion of the literature.

Chapter 4

The Chronicler's History of the Law Book

Research on the law *book* in the Chronicler's Work has been almost exclusively oriented toward two well-known passages, Ezra 7 and Nehemiah 8. The former, according to the standard interpretation, describes the commission Ezra received from Artaxerxes (I or II) to transport the law book from Babylon to Judah, where he was to teach and enforce it. Nehemiah 8, then, is taken to be the account of Ezra's promulgation of the law book by a public reading. Given this consensus, the questions that have exercised scholars for more than a century are two: First, when did this take place? and second, what exactly were the contents of the book? The history of the attempt to answer these questions makes for interesting reading, but it is not within the scope of this chapter. Suffice it to say that neither question has been resolved.

It is somewhat surprising, however, in light of the Chronicler's long-recognized preference for theological rigor over historical accuracy, that the historicity of the events just mentioned has been accepted without challenge.[1]   More surprising is it still when one considers that Ezra 7 cannot be said unambiguously to support its standard interpretation. In the first place, while references to a law *book* or *written* law are frequent in the Chronicler's Work, the law in Ezra's hand, identified in Ezra 7 as the "law of Moses," "law of YHWH," "law of the God of Heaven," "law of your God" and "wisdom of your God," is not identified as a book or as written law. Secondly, בידך in v. 14 with reference to the law and in v. 25 to the wisdom of God need not be taken

---

[1] Torrey, who denies the historicity of Ezra, is an exception. Cf. Torrey, *Ezra Studies*, pp. 240-48.

literally.[2]   We find the equivalent term elsewhere in the Chronicler's History (in no case derived from Kings) at 1 Chron. 24:19 (ביר אהרן) and 2 Chron. 33:8 and 34:14 (ביד משה). In each of these cases it is clear that something other than literal material possession in one's hands is meant. The *RSV*, for example, translates the term as "given through" or "established by," thus indicating Moses or Aaron's function or authority. And it is precisely Ezra's skill, dedication, and authority with reference to the law that is stressed in Ezra 7. Now while it follows from this that Ezra is sent to teach the law, if not actually to deliver the law book, the text makes clear that the Chronicler does not conceive this law to be entirely new to the Judeans. Ezra's orders are indeed to teach those who do not know the laws, but his first task is to appoint judges to judge all those who already do know them (7:25-26).

Finally, certain material goods are said to have been entrusted to Ezra for delivery to Jerusalem and, typically, the Chronicler records that Ezra fulfilled this task (Ezra 8:31-36). On the other hand, no clear statement is made to the effect that Ezra was to convey to Judah a book of law, and no text records that he ever did. Is this because the book of law was less valued than the silver, gold and other goods or because the Chronicler did not in fact imagine the law book to be in Babylon (not in Judah) and therefore requiring transportation? If the latter be the case, then the questions of when Ezra introduced the law book and what exactly its contents were disappear.

Having already discussed the mission of Ezra from an historical perspective.[3] I do not wish here to pursue these historical issues, but rather to raise a question about the Chronicler's understanding of the history of Israelite religion, in particular the history of its book of law. The question is this: What does the Chronicler's Work claim or imply to be the origin and subsequent history of the Torah book, and how has that book functioned (according to the Chronicler) during the course of its history?

---

[2] Francis Brown, Samuel Rolles Driver and Charles A. Briggs, *A Hebrew and English Lexicon of the Old Testament* (Oxford, 1907), p. 391a.

[3] Cf. pp. 31-39.

The History of the Torah Book
According to the Chronicler's History Work

Even the most perfunctory reading of the Chronicler's History will turn up a number of references to Torah, many of which refer more specifically to a written Torah.[4] A close examination of these latter references discloses the Chronicler's assumption of the existence of a book of law variously described as "the book of Moses," "the law of Moses," "the book of the law of Moses," "the law of God," "the law of YHWH," "the book of the law of YHWH," "the book of the law of God," "the book of the law," or simply "the book."[5] These titles appear to be interchangeable, but reveal the point which the Chronicler wished to stress: as a body of written Torah originating with the deity the book of law possesses superlative authority. It is to this authority that he appeals when on thirteen occasions he uses the formula ככתוב to describe the manner in which some (usually ritual) act was carried out.[6]

The Book of the Law in the Pre-state Period

The Chronicler does not provide an account of the origin of Torah, or of the book of Torah. There is no narrative of the events at Sinai.[7] Yet it seems clear from the many references to the book or law of Moses and the phrase, "The book of the law of YHWH in the hand of (*RSV*, given through) Moses" (2 Chron. 34:14), that the Chronicler assumed the existence, not just of Torah, but of a Torah book since the time of Moses.

---

[4] Myers, *I Chronicles.* p. LXIII, notes that the Chronicler places more stress on Torah than did his deuteronomistic *Vorlage.*

[5] 2 Chron. 25:4; 35:12; Ezra 6:18; Neh. 13:1 (the book of Moses). 2 Chron. 23:18; 30:16; Ezra 3:2 (the law of Moses). Neh. 8:1 (the book of the law of Moses). Neh. 8:8 (the law of God). 1 Chron. 16:40; 2 Chron. 31:3; 35:26 (the law of YHWH). 2 Chron. 17:9; 34:14; Neh. 9:3 (the book of the law of YHWH). Neh. 8:18 (the book of the law of God). 2 Chron. 34:15; Neh. 8:3 (the book of the law). 2 Chron. 34:15, 16, 21, 24; Neh. 8:5, 8 (the book).

[6] 2 Chron. 23:18; 25:4; 30:5, 18; 31:3; 35:12, 26; Ezra 3:2, 4; 6:18 (Aramaic); Neh. 8:15; 10:35, 37. Cf. 1 Chron. 16:40 (לכל־הכתוב) and 2 Chron. 34:21 (ככל־הכתוב).

[7] But cf. Neh. 9:13-14.

The Book of the Law in the Period of the Judean Monarchy

The Chronicler's narrative proper begins with the rise of the Judean monarchy. It focuses especially on the career of David, who, we are told, left Zadok the priest and his brethren before the tabernacle at Gibeon to offer the *Tamid* לכל־הכתוב בתורת יהוה (1 Chron. 16:39-40). This is the first reference in the Chronicler's History to written Torah. But as we have just remarked, the Chronicler assumed the book to have been around since Moses and therefore to have been available to David, who, of course, acknowledged its authority and acted in accordance with its instructions.

The next reference to a *written* Torah is in connection with the reign of Jehoshaphat. David, however, is said to have charged Solomon to "keep the Torah of YHWH your God" (1 Chron. 22:12), which he apparently did. Rehoboam, however, forsook the "torah of YHWH" (2 Chron 12:1). Abijah claims that Judah, unlike Israel, is faithful to YHWH (2 Chron. 13:8-12), while Asa commanded Judah to keep the Torah (2 Chron. 14:4) and is credited with a religious reform (not mentioned in Kings) which was bolstered by the prophetic words of Azariah to the effect that Israel's long period without the true God, a teaching priest, or Torah was ended (2 Chron. 15:1-7).

We come next to Jehoshaphat, who early in his reign, according to 2 Chron. 17:7-9, sent five of his princes together with nine Levites and two priests to teach throughout the cities of Judah. What they taught is not stated but is nevertheless clear from the phrase "having the book of the law with them" (v. 9). This tradition is not found in Kings, but neither is it the creation of the Chronicler as the priority of the laymen and the secondary and Chronistic nature of v. 8 shows.[8]   The Chronicler, it follows, had a text which affirmed the existence of a book of law and itinerant lay teachers of it. With slight modification the text was made to conform to the Chronicler's anachronistic assumptions about the roles of priests and Levites. It was then put to use as a part of his overall conviction that the history of Judah could be evaluated in terms of the requirements of the law book in existence since Mosaic times and that the fortunes of the nation were determined by the comportment of the king.

---

[8] Williamson, *1 and 2 Chronicles*, p. 282.

Jehoshaphat's pious initiative in sending teachers of the law to the people was but a part of his faithfulness. In addition, he removed the high places and the *Asherim* (17:6) and appointed judges to "decide disputed cases" and to instruct the people "concerning bloodshed, law or commandment, statutes or ordinances" (2 Chron. 19:4-11). In consequence of this faithfulness, but only while Jehoshaphat remained faithful, Judah enjoyed peace and stability.

Jehoshaphat was followed in turn by Jehoram, Ahaziah and then the usurper Athaliah. The Chronicler notes that each did evil in the sight of YHWH, but makes no mention of the law book in connection with their reigns.

With the successful coup of the priest Jehoiada, however, the child Joash was crowned in place of his grandmother, and the law book reappeared. Jehoiada, as vice-regent for the child king, initiated a covenant and a religious reform that included the destruction of the idolatrous temple, altars, and images, the execution of the priest of Baal, and the restoration of the Yahwistic temple personnel and sacrificial ritual "as it is written in the law of Moses" (2 Chron. 23:18).

What had been the fate of the law book in the years from Jehoshaphat to Jehoiada? Of this the Chronicler says nothing specific. It had not ceased to exist, however, so one can assume that it was simply ignored. For this king and people suffered greatly.

Amaziah succeeded Joash and immediately avenged his father's assassination. He did not execute the children of Joash's killers, however, because "the law in the book of Moses" (2 Chron. 25:4) forbade it. The Chronicler therefore assumed that the law book was being read and its authority recognized in the period of Amaziah. Interestingly, this appears to be the Chronicler's only direct quotation of the law book; it quotes Deut. 24:16, but the Chronicler is following his Deuteronomic *Vorlage* (2 Kgs. 14:2-6).

The next reference to a law book or written law occurs in connection with the reform of Hezekiah, the fourth Judean monarch following Amaziah. Hezekiah's immediate predecessor, the thoroughly evil Ahaz, not only failed to discourage idolatry, but actually closed the temple and built high places throughout Judah for idolatrous worship. It was against this backdrop that the Chronicler narrated, in light of his own ideals, the reform of Hezekiah.

According to the Chronicler (2 Chron. 29-32), Hezekiah was responsible for a major religious reform which included an unprecedented festival along with a centralized Passover celebration which was not mentioned in Kings. Whether this in fact took place or is an invention of the Chronicler based on the prior celebration of Solomon and the subsequent Passover of Josiah has been much discussed.[9]   Our present concern, however, is to trace the Chronicler's understanding of the history of the written law or law book, and for that task the chapters on Hezekiah are especially helpful. They highlight several of the Chronicler's major theological concerns-- as a comparison with the Kings version will show-- and lend clear support to the thesis that the Chronicler believed the law book existed long before his own time, and that the fate of the people was determined in strict retributive fashion according to their obedience of its commandments.

The Chronicler begins by noting that immediately on his ascension to the throne Hezekiah opened the temple doors closed by his father and proceeded to restore the temple, its personnel, and the covenant with Yahweh. This we are told (in the form of a speech by Hezekiah) was intended to turn the anger of Yahweh away from Judah and Jerusalem which had suffered terribly because of the people's unfaithfulness (2 Chron. 29:3-10). The people responded to the king's initiative; they sanctified themselves and the temple, offered numerous sacrifices, and at the king's invitation assembled in Jerusalem to celebrate the Passover. The people then went throughout the cities of Judah, Benjamin, Ephraim and Manasseh, destroying high places and other idolatrous objects. When they had returned to their towns, they readily complied with the king's command that they support the clergy by a tithe. God rewarded their faithfulness with such an abundance of produce that storage space had to be prepared for the surfeit of their contributions. Finally, and this demonstrates how Hezekiah's reform had turned away Yahweh's wrath, when Sennacherib had thrown up a siege around Jerusalem, Hezekiah and Isaiah sought the help of Yahweh and he miraculously intervened. The Assyrians were routed, and their king returned in shame to his own land. But what about an authoritative text, a written law conformity to which determines one's desert? Interestingly, Kings, which attributes a religious reform to Hezekiah and actually goes beyond the Chronicler in praise of him (e.g., "He trusted in the Lord...there was none like him among all the kings of Judah after him, nor...before him," 2 Kgs. 18:5), has absolutely no reference to a written law or book of

---

[9] Cf. p. 110 n. 73.

law in connection with his reign. Chronicles, on the other hand, in its account of Hezekiah's reform uses the formulaic ‏ככתוב‎ with reference to the normative law of Moses or Yahweh three times.[10] The Chronicler, it follows, believed that the law book, while not obeyed since the reign of Amaziah--certainly not in the reign of Ahaz--had not been destroyed. It was available to Hezekiah and was the basis for his reform. His faithfulness was precisely obedience to this written law of Moses, and on the principle of retributive justice he earned a period of prosperity and protection from the Assyrians.

Hezekiah was followed by Manasseh and then Amon, both of whom practiced evil in the sight of Yahweh. In describing Manasseh's reign both 2 Kgs. 21:8-9 and 2 Chron. 33:8-9 quote Yahweh's speech to David and Solomon in which he stressed that possession of the land was conditional. It depended on keeping the Torah of Moses. Both texts note that Manasseh seduced the populace into evil greater than that of the nations Yahweh "destroyed before the people of Israel." But neither Kings nor Chronicles refers to written Torah in the course of their accounts of Manasseh's or Amon's reigns. The deuteronomistic writer, nevertheless, explained the fall of Judah as punishment for Manasseh's sins (2 Kgs. 21:10-15; 23:26-27), while the Chronicler accounted for Manasseh's long reign with the story of his repentance and attempted religious reform (2 Chron. 33:10-17). Amon, however, did not repent and was assassinated (2 Chron. 33:21-24).

Amon's eight-year old son Josiah was made king, and, as is well known, the book of the law figures prominently in both the Kings and Chronicles versions of his reign. In fact, for much of his account the Chronicler has virtually reproduced the narrative in Kings. In both accounts, the law book is taken to have been Josiah's authority, on how to keep Passover for example (cf. 2 Kgs. 23:21, 2 Chron. 35:12), and is the standard against which Josiah's deeds are specifically judged (2 Kgs. 23:25, 2 Chron. 35:26).

The two accounts also have some differences. The Chronicler, for example, not surprisingly has "priests and Levites" (2 Chron. 34:30) where Kings reads "priests and prophets" (2 Kgs. 23:2), and felt it necessary to provide a theological reason for Josiah's premature demise. But of more significance in the present context are the following:

---

[10] 2 Chron. 30:5, 18; 31:3.

1) In Kings (2 Kgs. 22-23) we are told nothing specific about events in Josiah's reign prior to his busy eighteenth regnal year, during which the law book was discovered, a covenant made, land and temple purged, and a centralized Passover kept in Jerusalem. According to Chronicles (2 Chron. 34-35), however, Josiah began "to seek the God of his father David" (34:3) in the eighth year of his reign, and four years later undertook a religious reform which was already accomplished when, in his eighteenth year, the law book was discovered.

2) It may be that the Chronicler thinks of the book of law as a longer work than the author of Kings did.[11] At any rate the Chronicler (2 Chron. 34:18) has "Shaphan read *from* it" (ויקרא־בו) for Kings' (2 Kgs. 22:10) "Shaphan read it" (ויקראהו), and simply omits the phrase "and he read it" (ויקראהו) in his version of 2 Kgs. 22:8 (cf. 2 Chron. 34:15). This might indicate that the Chronicler thought the book too long to read in its entirety. On the other hand, both Kings and Chronicles later in their narratives claim that Josiah read "all the words of the book of the covenant which had been found in the house of the Lord" (2 Kgs. 23:2; 2 Chron. 34:30).

Whatever its historical basis, the Chronicler's account of a Josianic reform prior to the discovery of the book of law raises several questions about his view of the function and history of the book. How could Josiah reform Judean religious practice without the guidance of the law book? Has the Chronicler in the process of underlining Josiah's piety undermined the importance of the book? Or is it simply the case that the book was not as important to the Chronicler as it appeared to have been in other texts? Or, again, did the Chronicler assume that the contents of the book were or should have been generally known and that the people were accountable for its contents whether or not the book itself was misplaced? Both the Kings and Chronicles versions of this episode support this last possibility since Josiah, on hearing the book, was greatly distressed because "great is the wrath of the Lord that is poured out on us, because our fathers have not kept the word of the Lord, to do according to all that is written in his book" (2 Chron. 34:21, cf. 2

---

[11] Curtis and Madsen, *Chronicles*, p. 508. Cf. Myers, *Ezra. Nehemiah*, p. 153.

Kgs. 22:13). Clearly the people are judged according to the requirements of the book whether the book is lost or found.

This, however, leads to a second problem: Why is Josiah distressed? The sequence in Kings makes sense: Josiah came to the throne in a period of apostasy; the law book was found and read to him; it apparently stated both the requirements of the covenant with Yahweh and the consequences of non-fulfillment; Josiah was greatly distressed and launched a reform in order to comply with the terms of the book. In Chronicles, however, the reform is before the discovery of the book and yet the king mourns. Why? An obvious explanation is that the Chronicler adapted the Kings version without noting the difficulties his redactional activity caused. Thomas Willi suggests another explanation. Writing on the Chronicler's conception of Torah, he argues that for the Chronicler *Torah* included more than the *book* of Torah.[12] In this he is surely correct. One of the texts he uses is 2 Chron. 34:19 as compared to its *Vorlage* (2 Kgs. 22:11). The Kings text says that "when the king (i.e. Josiah) heard the words of the *book* of the law, he rent his clothes." The Chronicler, Willi points out, wrote that the king rent his clothes when he heard "the words of the law." The Chronicler has omitted the reference to a *book*, he argues, because Torah is more than the book which contains Torah.[13] Unfortunately, this interpretation, while supporting the view I favor--namely, that the Chronicler assumed Torah to be known and normative whether or not the Torah book was lost--puts too much weight on what is in context a minor redactional difference. That is, 2 Kgs. 22:8-23:25 refers to the new-found Torah as a book or a written Torah eleven times. And while the Chronicler omitted the word "book" in the verse just mentioned (v. 19) and did not reproduced 2 Kgs. 23:24 (which includes "the words of the law which were written in the book"), he also managed in the same context (2 Chron. 34:14-35:19) to refer to the Torah as a book eleven times.

An equally minor deviation from Kings at 2 Chron. 34:24 (cf. 2 Kgs. 22:16) may provide a more reliable indication of the Chronicler's understanding of Josiah's distress. In Kings the prophetess authenticates the book and sends a message to the king: "Thus says the Lord, Behold I will bring evil upon this place and upon its inhabitants, all the words of the book which the king of

---

[12] Thomas Willi, "Thora in den biblischen Chronikbüchern, *Judaica* XXXVI (1980) 102-105, 148-51.

[13] Willi, "Thora," p. 105.

Judah has read." The Chronicles text is very similar but has "all the curses" in places of Kings' "all the words." Perhaps the Chronicler's notion is that Josiah knew well enough what the law required even before the text was found, but that only after hearing the book did he know the terrible consequences that generations of idolatry were about to produce. On the other hand, the Chronicler's point may simply be that it was not the words of the law that upset Josiah--he, after all, was a pious king who loved the law--but rather the curses that were included in the book. All that can be said with confidence is that here as elsewhere in the Chronicler's History it is assumed that the Torah is known, or should be, even if the book of Torah is not. And that seems to be its fate. Having just been rediscovered, the book is not mentioned again until the period of the restoration.

The Book of the Law in the Period of the Restoration

In its present form, Ezra-Nehemiah describes the sequence of the restoration of the Judean community as follows: 1) an initial period of restoration of cult and temple; 2) Ezra's mission to enforce and teach Torah; and 3) Nehemiah's administration during which Ezra publicly read the law book. In each of these periods decisive actions are described and claimed to have been taken ככתוב. We will trace the history of the book of law as best we can through each of these periods, but on the assumption that the Nehemiah material was originally independent and only secondarily associated with the Ezra tradition, the two will be treated separately.

1)   The initial restoration:

For the Chronicler the edict of Cyrus authorizing a Judean restoration marks the start of a new beginning in the history of Israel's relationship to Yahweh. By the Chronicler's reckoning, over forty-thousand people took immediate advantage of this opportunity, and returned to Jerusalem and Judah (Ezra 1-2). In the seventh month (presumably of the first year of the return), the returnees having settled in their towns, the priest Jeshua and Zerubbabel rebuilt the altar in order to offer burnt offerings (Ezra 3:1-3). This first step toward a restored religious community was taken, we are told, ככתוב בתורת־משה (v. 2). Thereafter the people

made all the required daily and seasonal offerings,[14] kept Sukkoth
ככתוב (3:4), and began to rebuild the temple. Despite local
opposition, they completed the project in the sixth year of Darius'
reign (515 B.C.E.). They then dedicated the temple, reestablished
the clerical orders ככתב ספר משה (6:18),[15] and kept the Passover.

2) Ezra's mission:
At this point the Chronicler introduces Ezra and his
commission from Artaxerxes, a copy of which (he claims) is
provided in the text (Ezra 7). I have already noted my skepticism
with regard to the common assumption that Ezra brought a book of
law to Judah.[16] It is no accident, in my opinion, that while the
"law is mentioned eight times in Ch. 7 (תורה twice, דת six times), it
is never said to be a book or in writing. The Chronicler's
assumption, as I have just shown, was that the book of law
preceded Ezra to Judah. It was, after all, the authority in accord
with which Ezra's predecessors had reestablished the cult of
Yahweh in Jerusalem.

Ezra's task, then, is not to deliver and introduce a new law
book, but rather to enforce and teach "the laws of your God" (v.
25). Were these laws new to the Judeans, one might expect the
order of his assignments to be reversed. It is not new law,
however, and so the Chronicler turns immediately to Ezra's
marriage reforms.

His account of Ezra's teaching role, and the next reference to
the law book, occurs in Neh. 8-9 (a text many scholars would place
following Ezra 8).[17] On the first day of the seventh month at a
huge outdoor assembly, Ezra read from the law book from dawn
until midday. He stood above the people flanked by thirteen men on
a platform erected for the occasion. The meaning of מפרש in our text
(Neh. 8:8) is obscure, but apparently the Levites interpreted the text
to aid the people's understanding.[18] The next day the heads of

---

[14] The Sabbath observance has been accidently omitted; cf. 1 Esdras 5:52 and
Ackroyd, *1 and 2 Chronicles, Ezra, Nehemiah*, p. 224.

[15] There is no pentateuchal text to which this could refer, cf. pp. 117-18.

[16] Cf. pp. 35-36, 73-74.

[17] Cf. pp. 31-34.

[18] Ackroyd, *1 and 2 Chronicles, Ezra, Nehemiah*, pp. 295-96. Myers, *Ezra.
Nehemiah*, p. 154, understands the verse to mean that the Levites translated
Ezra's Hebrew into Aramaic, and cites Paul Kahle, *The Cairo Geniza* (London,

families, the priests and the Levites joined Ezra to study the book. In doing so they discovered the instructions for the autumn festival, which they kept in accordance with the stipulations of the law book (Neh. 8:13-18). There follows in Nehemiah 9:1-5 a description of a day of mournful fasting, during which the Israelites separated themselves from foreigners, confessed their sins, and read from the book of the law. The date of this event is given as "the twenty-fourth day of this month" (v. 1), but the month is not named. Neither is Ezra, and it may be that the text is out of place or is a parallel version of Ezra's reading of the law (Neh. 8:1-12).[19] It seems clear, however, that the Chronicler intended, whatever the historical reality, to include both Sukkoth and a Day of Atonement in the seventh month.[20]

In its present form the Ezra narrative of Neh. 8-9 is brought to completion by Neh. 10 with its account of a covenant made by the people to keep the law, and in particular to support the restored temple cult by, among other things, providing the wood offering and first fruits ככתוב (vv. 35, 37). A number of scholars, however, have argued that Ch. 10 should be included with the Nehemiah material and placed after Neh. 13.[21] There are two reasons for this. In the first place, Nehemiah is named at the head of the list of signatories to the covenant while Ezra goes unmentioned. Batten

---

1947), p. 124, who argued what the rabbis believed (cf. b. Megillah 3a), namely, that the Targum goes back to Ezra.

[19] Ackroyd, *1 and 2 Chronicles, Ezra, Nehemiah*, p. 300.

[20] Smith, *Palestinian Parties*, pp. 123, 273, notes that Ezra's Law "did not provide for observance of the Day of Atonement." Of this text he says only that it is an editorial addition (p. 251). Blenkinsopp, "Sectarianism," p. 6 n. 22, makes the point that the fast in Neh. 9 on the twenty-fourth day of the seventh month is not the fast of the Day of Atonement, which is dated by H (Lev. 23:27-32) and P (Lev. 16:29-34) on the tenth day of the seventh month. Ackroyd, *1 and 2 Chronicles, Ezra, Nehemiah*, p. 299, points out that "the precise dating of annual celebrations appears to be later than their origin" (a fact borne out by my investigation of Sukkoth and Mazzoth, see below). The date in P (Lev. 16:29), he thinks, is later than the preceding description of the fast. On this basis he believes Neh. 9:1-5 may indicate that the date of the Day of Atonement was not yet fixed in Ezra's time. On the other hand, "(A) fast could be proclaimed on an appropriate day if there was need (cf. Joel 2:15), and Zech. 8:19 refers to fasts celebrated in the fourth, fifth, seventh and tenth months of the year."

[21] E.g., Myers, *Ezra. Nehemiah*, p. 174; cf. Bowman, *Ezra and Nehemiah*, p. 757.

pointed out long ago that Ezra would not likely have been a bystander,[22] and Bowman makes the obvious suggestion that, had the Chronicler wished to conclude the Ezra story with Ch. 10, he would have named Ezra instead of Nehemiah at 10:2 (Ev. 10:1).[23] On the other hand, the entire list of names looks like an interpolation to Ackroyd, who points out that Ezra's name is also lacking in Ch. 9.[24] The other reason for taking Neh. 10 as a part of the Nehemiah material is the purported great similarity between the activities related in Chs. 10 and 13. Bowman, for example, regards Ch. 10 (not including the list of names) as a summary of the events described in Neh. 13 and thus not a part of the Ezra story.[25] Ackroyd allows that the Chronicler or a later editor may have used a narrative originally associated with Nehemiah to end his account of Ezra's activity, but argues that Ch. 10 more likely derives from independent material associated with neither Ezra nor Nehemiah which the Chronicler put to its present use.[26] In his view Ch. 13, which differs from the rest of the Nehemiah narrative, was based on the same or similar material. Nehemiah 10, then, while perhaps not originally a description of Ezra's work, is best understood as representing the Chronicler's view of the completion of Ezra's mission in which, as we have seen, the law book figures prominently.

3) Nehemiah's administration:
I have taken the view that the Nehemiah material was an addition to the Chronicler's History Work. The one text, however, that mentions the law book in connection with Nehemiah's administration is consistent with the Chronicler's view of the function and authority of the written law. That text, Neh. 13:1-3, describes a public reading of the law (apparently Deut. 23:4-6, Ev. vv. 3-5.) and the consequent separation of Israel from "those of foreign descent" (v. 3). The text does not actually mention Nehemiah and may originally have been an Ezra tradition;

---

[22] Batten, *The Books of Ezra and Nehemiah*, p. 352.

[23] Bowman, *Ezra and Nehemiah*, p. 757.

[24] Ackroyd, *1 and 2 Chronicles, Ezra, Nehemiah*, p. 305; (MT lacks the reference to Ezra at Neh. 9:6).

[25] Cf. Bowman, *Ezra and Nehemiah*, p. 757, which surveys a range of views.

[26] Ackroyd, *1 and 2 Chronicles, Ezra, Nehemiah*, p. 305.

nevertheless, it seems clear from the context that the editor took this event to have occurred under Nehemiah's governorship.[27]

Conclusion

In light of this survey of the Chronicler's references to the book of the Torah, we may return to the question posed at the outset, namely: What does the Chronicler's Work claim or imply to be the origin and subsequent history of the Torah book, and how has that book functioned during the course of its history? We have seen that the Chronicler believed the Torah book had possessed divine authority and provided normative instruction since its origins in Mosaic times. The entire History Work, moreover, testifies to his conviction that all of Judean history was determined in retributive fashion by the people's (especially the leaders') obedience or disobedience of those instructions. Indeed, the law book itself, as Josiah learned (2 Chron. 34:24), contained all the curses that would and did follow non-compliance. The Chronicler believed that like Judah the book of the law had survived a checkered history, having been at times lost, found, forgotten, and taught. Finally, under the Golah leadership, especially under Ezra, it was restored to its proper place in the post-exilic community, which was itself (he believed) restored according to all that is written in the book of the law of Moses.

---

[27] Myers, *Ezra. Nehemiah*, p. 207, and Rudolph, *Esra und Nehemia*, p. 202, point out that Neh. 13:3 cannot refer to the results of Ezra's activity since Neh. 9:2 already has. Bowman, *Ezra and Nehemiah*, p. 802, makes the same point (although he mistakenly cites Ezra 9:2 for Neh. 9:2).

Chapter 5

The Chronicler's Use of Pentateuchal Legislation

We have seen that the Chronicler in his retelling of Judah's history consistently assumes that the book of the law of Moses available in his own day had originated in Mosaic times and was or should have been known and obeyed ever since. That it was not always known or obeyed, on his interpretation, is the explanation for every unfortunate event in the history of the covenant people. If, however, it seems certain that such a book or written law existed in the Chronicler's day, it is not certain what exactly it contained.

In this chapter, I turn to an analysis of the texts in which the Chronicler cites the written law as the authority which required or forbade some specific act, ceremony or institution. The question which I address to these texts is: What is the relationship between the Chronicler's description of the law book's requirements and the requirements of extant codes of pentateuchal legislation? Is the Chronicler's law book the Pentateuch, the Holiness Code, Deuteronomy, or something else?

That the book at least included Deuteronomy seems apparent from the one occasion that the Chronicler cites "the book of Moses" (2 Chron. 25:4) and goes on to quote from it. The passage explains why Amaziah, in avenging the assassination of his father, killed the perpetrators but not their children, namely: "The law in the book of Moses" includes the Deuteronomic stipulation that children not be put to death for the sins of their fathers (Deut. 24:16).[1]   On the other hand, the Chronicler's dependence on the Priestly legislation

---

[1] The Chronicles text, however, is dependent on its *Vorlage* (2 Kgs. 14:6), which also quotes Deut. 24:16.

was recognized at least as early as Wellhausen[2] and is today beyond dispute. One may cite, for example, the reference to the tax levied by Moses for the tent of testimony (2 Chron. 24:6) which depends on Ex. 30:11-16,[3] or 2 Chron. 26:17-18 where the Chronicler has expanded the deuteronomistic account of Uzziah's leprosy (2 Kgs. 15:5) by supplying the reason for his illness. He had entered the temple intending to burn incense to Yahweh on the altar of incense, a violation of the Priestly stipulation that only the sons of Aaron could do so (Ex. 30:1-10, Num. 17:5, Ev. 16:40). When reminded of this fact by Azariah and eighty of his fellow priests, the king, unrepentant, responded in anger and broke out in leprosy.

In addition to such rather straightforward texts which depend on either D or P, there are other occasions when the Chronicler has combined Deuteronomic and Priestly laws together with regulations not found in the final form of the Pentateuch and cited the whole without distinction as deriving from the written law of Moses. A good example of this procedure may be found in Neh. 10:29-39 (Ev. 10:28-38), a text, as we have seen, which the Chronicler used to round off the Ezra narrative. In this text all those who had "separated themselves from the peoples of the lands to the Torah of God" (v. 29) bound themselves by an oath to keep this written law given by Moses (vv. 30, 35, 37). Several specific obligations are listed, as follows:

1) v. 31; the obligation not to intermarry with the peoples of the land. This depends verbally as well as conceptually on D (Deut. 7:3).

2) v. 32a; the obligation to refrain from trading on the Sabbath. The ancient code (Ex. 20:8-11; cf. 23:12), P (Ex. 31:12-17), H (Lev. 23:3), and D (Deut. 5:12-15) all proscribed work on the Sabbath; none makes special reference to trade, but, as Amos 8:5 indicates, not buying or selling was from early times taken to be a part of keeping the Sabbath.

3) v. 32b; the obligation to observe a sabbatical year in which crops would be left unharvested and debts would be forgiven. The Holiness Code (Lev. 25:1-7), like the older JE (Ex. 23:10), stipulates the sabbatical release of

---

[2] Wellhausen, *Prolegomena*, pp. 171-72.

[3] The *Vorlage* of 2 Chron. 24 (2 Kgs. 12) refers to an assessment on the people, but not to a tax levied by Moses.

crops, but says nothing about the forgiveness of debts. On the other hand, D requires a sabbatical year in which debts are forgiven (Deut. 15:1-2), but says nothing about leaving crops unharvested.

4)   v. 33; the obligation to pay an annual temple tax of one third of a shekel. According to P (Ex. 30:13) the tax for the sanctuary was to be a half shekel. The change from a half to a third shekel "may be explained by the fact that the Persian monetary system was based on ten silver shekels for one gold shekel, whereas the sacred shekel was in the proportion of fifteen to one."[4] If this is the case, the people have obligated themselves to pay the tax required by P.[5] If on the other hand, because of the poverty of the restoration community they have actually obligated themselves to less than the Priestly requirement, then they have violated the P law that the half shekel tax not be reduced for the poor or raised for the rich (Ex. 30:15).

5)   v. 35; the obligation to contribute the wood offering. Although this is specifically identified as a requirement of the written law, the Pentateuch contains no corresponding legislation.

6)   vv. 36-38; the obligation of the first fruits and tithes. The signatories of the oath vowed to give the first fruits to the priests and the tithes to the Levites. According to Deuteronomic law (Deut. 18:1-4; 26:1-4) the due of the Levitical priests (priests and Levites not being distinguished) was a part of the sacrifice and the first fruits. The tithe is not normally given to the Levites, but is to be eaten in celebration by the people (Deut. 14:22-26). Every third year, however, the tithe is to be shared by Levites, sojourners, the fatherless and widows (Deut. 14:28-29). In contrast, the Priestly code, with which our Nehemiah text agrees, allocates the first fruits to the priests and the tithes to the Levites (Num. 18:8-13, 21, 24).

---

[4] Myers, *Ezra. Nehemiah*, pp. 178-79; cf. Blenkinsopp, "Sectarianism," p. 6, who dates Ex. 30:11-16 after Neh. 10:33 "given the inexorable tendency for taxation to increase."

[5] Ackroyd, *1 and 2 Chronicles, Ezra, Nehemiah*, p. 307, has noted that Ex. 30:11-13 does not specify that the tax is to be paid annually. It may be "a once-for-all payment."

7)   v. 39; the Levites' obligation of the tithe of the tithes. Only in Num. 18:26 (P) do we find this requirement.

What this survey makes clear is that no simple identification of the Chronicler's law book as Deuteronomy, the Priestly code, or the Pentateuch can be made. Instead we must investigate and describe in detail the legal material in the Chronicler's Work and the variety of its relationships to the several collections of pentateuchal legislation.

Given the Chronicler's long recognized emphasis on the proper practice of Judaism, it is not surprising that in the vast majority of instances he uses the formulaic ככתוב, or otherwise claims the authority of the written law, in contexts where he is dealing with some aspect of the sacrificial cult. In the rest of this chapter I will describe these instances under the following headings: The Required Burnt Offerings, Sukkoth, Passover and Unleavened Bread, and The Official Functions of Cultic Personnel. The chapter will conclude with an analysis of the rather different relationship to pentateuchal legislation that is present in the Nehemiah Memoir.

The Required Burnt Offerings

The Chronicler's History includes a number of texts which describe aspects of the regular required sacrificial ritual. In the section which follows I will treat several such texts which, in addition, note explicitly that the procedures narrated are required by previous legislation. This legislation is variously described as originating with the deity, or Moses, or both; the conception clearly is of a body of law provided to Israel by YHWH through the mediation of Moses, which is available in written form.

2 Chronicles 31:3
Having introduced the reign of Hezekiah and narrated his cleansing of the temple and the subsequent Passover festival, the Chronicler in 2 Chron. 31:2-11 states that Hezekiah established the divisions of the priests and Levites according to their roles in the cultus. In this context the Chronicler found occasion to note 1) that the king provided from his own property for the burnt offerings (עלות), 2) that regular burnt offerings were made on each morning and evening, Sabbath, new moon, and on the appointed feasts, and 3) that these offerings (and perhaps the king's contributions) were made ככתוב בתורת יהוה.

The question to what exactly the last phrase of the verse refers cannot be resolved simply by noting that no extant text places the demand of v. 3a on the king.[6] Yet the sentence is ambiguous; clearly the list of sacrificial occasions is regarded as being according to Torah, but the fact of the king's contribution is not treated as novel or unwarranted. The tenor of the whole treatment of Hezekiah is that he was a reformer not an innovator. We will return to that point, but first I wish to deal with the question of the Chronicler's sources for this passage.

    In the first place, in his treatment of the reign of Hezekiah the Chronicler has greatly expanded the narrative of the Deuteronomistic Historian. And while he may have had historical source documents for some of the material not drawn from 2 Kgs. 18,[7] the note at 2 Chron. 31:3, not found in Kings, can be recognized as the composition of the Chronicler for several reasons. 2 Kings 18:6 had stated that Hezekiah "kept the commandments which the Lord commanded Moses;" the Chronicler expanded the narrative in keeping with his theological interest in the cultus to specify the commandments which Hezekiah had kept. In addition, the Chronicler viewed Hezekiah, the reformer, as a second Solomon (cf. 2 Chron. 30:26).[8] According to 2 Chron. 8:12-13, an expansion of 1 Kgs. 9:25, Solomon had offered burnt offerings, כמצות משה, "for the Sabbaths, the new moons, and the three annual feasts" (cf. 2 Chron. 2:3, Ev. 2:4). According to 2 Chron. 31:3, Hezekiah acted similarly.

    Our text states that Hezekiah provided for the burnt offerings "from his own possessions." As Rudolph noted, the law did not require this of the king;[9] it is not in fact required by any text in the Hebrew Bible. Curtis and Madsen, however, associate the Chronicler's description with the requirement of Ezekiel's program that the prince (הנשיא) furnish the sacrificial material (Ezek. 45:17).[10] But the text in Ezekiel does not state that the prince is to provide "from his own possessions" but rather in the immediately

---

[6] Rudolph, *Chronikbücher*, pp. 304, 306.

[7] Jacob M. Myers, *II Chronicles. Introduction, Translation, and Notes*, The Anchor Bible XIII (Garden City, 1965), p. 176.

[8] Williamson, *Israel*, pp. 119-25; Myers, *II Chronicles*, pp. 179, 183; Rudolph, *Chronikbücher*, pp. 303, 307.

[9] Rudolph, *Chronikbücher*, pp. 304, 306.

[10] Curtis and Madsen, *Chronicles*, pp. 478-79.

preceding verses (45:13-16) places the obligation on the people: they are to provide the prince, who then apportions the provisions as the ritual requires.[11]

More certain results are obtainable in regard to the question of the provenance of the list of the occasions for burnt offerings found in 2 Chron. 31:3b, as follows: morning and evening, Sabbaths, new moons and appointed feasts. At least this list of occasions is said to be כככוב בחורת יהוה. While there are numerous texts in the Hebrew Bible which refer to some of these occasions, there is good reason to believe that the Chronicler is here following, and identifying as written law of YHWH, Num. 28-29. In the first place, Num. 28-29 lists the same sacrifices and in the same order as does 2 Chron. 31:3b, while no other pentateuchal text requires the Sabbath burnt offering. Ezekiel's program does require burnt offerings on the same occasions, including the Sabbath, but lists them differently. That is burnt offerings are to be made on the feasts (45:21-25; 46:11), on Sabbaths (46:4-5), new moons (46:6-7), and daily (46:13-15). Moreover, the daily sacrifice is offered each morning (as in Lev. 6:1-6, Ev. 6:8-13), and not each morning and evening as in our text[12] and Num. 28:3-8.[13]

According to Martin Noth, Num. 28-29 was not an original part of P.[14] It depends on exilic and post-exilic texts, in particular Lev. 1-7 and 23,[15] and while in *A History of Pentateuchal Traditions* he contents himself to argue that it is not possible to prove that Num. 28-29 (among other texts he discusses) was a supplement to P rather than to the "already combined Pentateuch,"[16] in his commentary on Numbers he describes Num. 28-29 as "from the literary point of view...an appendix to the Pentateuchal narrative...one of the latest sections of the Pentateuch."[17]

---

[11] Rudolph, *Chronikbücher*, p. 306.

[12] The daily morning and evening burnt offerings are also attributed to the written law in 1 Chron. 16:40 and Ezra 3:2-6.

[13] The late priestly Ex. 29:38-42a requires a morning and evening תמיד, but not the other occasions given in 2 Chron. 31:3 and Num. 28-29.

[14] Noth, *Überlieferungsgeschichtliche Studien I*, pp. 192-94, 217.

[15] Martin Noth, *Numbers: A Commentary*, The Old Testament Library, trans. James D. Martin (Philadelphia, 1968), p. 219.

[16] Noth, *Pentateuchal Traditions*, pp. 8-9.

[17] Noth, *Numbers*, p. 219.

Leaving aside the question of whether Num. 28-29 was added to P or to the combined Pentateuch, if Noth is right that it was a late addition, then, given our view that the Chronicler has made use of it and identified it as written Torah of YHWH, it follows that the Chronicler at least in this instance accords authoritative status to what is now a very late stratum of the Pentateuch.[18]

We noted above that the Chronicler viewed Hezekiah as a second Solomon, and that the commentators associated 2 Chron. 31:3 with 2 Chron. 2:3 (Ev. 2:4) and 2 Chron. 8:12-13. Both of these texts, to which we now turn, deal with Solomon's involvement in the sacrificial ritual.

2 Chronicles 2:3 (Ev. 2:4)

In 1 Kgs. 5:15-20 (Ev. 5:1-6) we have Solomon's message to Hiram king of Tyre that he will build a temple for the name of YHWH and his request that Hiram provide, at his own price, cedar for the project. This episode is taken up and expanded by the Chronicler in 2 Chron. 1:18-2:9 (Ev. 2:1-10). For our purposes, the most significant of the Chronicler's additions is the description of the ritual for which the proposed temple is intended, namely: "for the burning of incense of sweet spices before him (YHWH), and for the continual offering of the showbread, and for burnt offerings (עלות) morning and evening, on the Sabbaths and the new moons and the appointed feasts of the Lord our God, as ordained forever" (2 Chron. 2:3, Ev. 2:4). As in 2 Chron. 31:3b, the occasions for burnt offerings listed here correspond exactly to the late text at Num. 28-29 and to no other text in the Pentateuch. To this list, however, the Chronicler has prefixed material not derived from Num. 28-29, namely, the reference to the burning of incense and the continual offering of showbread. Instructions for the former are found in Ex. 30:1-10, a text added to P, which did not envision the post-exilic altar of incense.[19]   Similarly, as regards the showbread,[20] the Chronicler appears to depend on late priestly Torah, specifically,

---

[18] Neither Num. 28-29 nor the Chronicler's History can be dated precisely, but they come from the same general period. One cannot assume that the material in Num. 28-29 was incorporated in the Pentateuch prior to the composition of the Chronicler's History.

[19] Martin Noth, *Exodus: A Commentary*, The Old Testament Library, trans. J.S. Bowden (Philadelphia, 1962), pp. 234-35.

[20] מערכה (לחם) only in the Chronicler's History. Cf. 1 Chron. 9:32; 23:29; 28:16; 2 Chron. 2:3 (Ev. 2:4); 13:11; 29:18; but cf. Lev. 24:6, 7.

Lev. 24:1-9 which "presupposes--as is nowhere else the case in the Holiness Code--the P narrative" (i.e., Ex. 25-27).[21] In sum, the use to which Solomon intends to put the proposed temple (2 Chron. 2:3; Ev. 2:4) is in all its details mandated by late priestly instruction found in texts which were supplemental to P if not to the combined Pentateuch.

2 Chronicles 8:12-13

Having completed construction of the temple, referred to as בית זבח at 2 Chron. 7:12 (and nowhere else in the Hebrew Bible), Solomon "offered up burnt offerings (עלוֹת)[22] ...as the duty of each day required...for the Sabbaths, the new moons and the three annual feasts--the feast of Unleavened Bread, the feast of Weeks, and the feast of Tabernacles" (2 Chron. 8:12-13). All this, it is again stated, was done כמצות משה (2 Chron. 8:13).

While its influence is again readily apparent, this text diverges markedly from Num. 28-29. There, following the instructions for the תמיד, Sabbath, and monthly burnt offerings, complete details are provided for the sacrifices at the five (not three) annual festivals, namely: Passover/Unleavened Bread (treated as one, Num. 28:16-25), First Fruits/Weeks (likewise treated as one, Num. 28:26-31), New Year ("a day for you to blow the trumpets" cf. Lev. 23:24; Num. 29:1-6), the Day of Atonement ("afflict yourselves" cf. Lev. 23:27, 29; Num. 29:7-11) and finally, Sukkoth (Num. 29:12-38). As we have noted above, however, the "commandment of Moses" in our text (2 Chron. 8:12-13) requires but three annual feasts, specifically: Unleavened Break, Weeks and Sukkoth.[23] Distinguishing between חג, pilgrimage, ("feast" in *RSV*) and the more general מוֹעֵד, set feast, Driver[24] argues that the above were the three annual pilgrimage feasts as identified in Deut. 16:1-16 and

---

[21] Martin Noth, *Leviticus: A Commentary*, revised ed., The Old Testament Library, trans. J.E. Anderson (Philadelphia, 1977), p. 177.

[22] Not in the temple, however, for that would be unlawful. The Chronicler also omits his *Vorlage's* reference to Solomon offering incense (1 Kgs. 9:25), also a violation of the law (Ex. 30:1-10), and the cause of Uzziah's leprosy (2 Chron. 26:16-21). Cf. Williamson, *1 and 2 Chronicles*, pp. 231-32.

[23] The *Vorlage* states that Solomon offered up burnt offerings three times a year, but does not name the occasions (cf. 1 Kgs. 9:25).

[24] Samuel Rolles Driver, *A Critical and Exegetical Commentary on Deuteronomy*, The International Critical Commentary (New York, 1895), pp. 188-89.

the earlier Ex. 23:14-19 and 34:18-24. In providing instruction for the burnt offering במוֹעדו (Num. 28:2), including daily, weekly, monthly and yearly sacrifices, Num. 28-29 identifies the same three occasions (Unleavened Bread, Weeks and Sukkoth, and those three alone) as חגים. It would seem possible, therefore, that in 2 Chron. 8:12-13 the Chronicler is indeed continuing to follow Num. 28-29. But closer examination suggests otherwise.

In the first place, while the מוֹעדים at which Solomon intends burnt offerings to be made go unspecified both as to number and name in 2 Chron. 2:3 (Ev. 2:4), when the temple is completed and Solomon sees his intentions fulfilled (2 Chron. 8:12-13), the מוֹעדים are stated to be three in number and are further identified specifically as the חגים of Unleavened Bread, Weeks, and Sukkoth. Secondly, the older cultic calendars of JE and especially D provide closer parallels to the list of חגים identified as the "three annual feasts" in 2 Chron. 8:13.

Exodus 23:14-19[25] lists the same three occasions, each identified as a feast (חג), but uses the earlier designations: feast of Harvest (for Weeks) and feast of Ingathering (for Sukkoth). The Yahwist (Ex. 34:18, 22), likewise identifies three חגים: Unleavened Bread, Weeks (using the more recent terminology), and Ingathering. Only in Deuteronomy (16:1-16; see especially v. 16) do we have the three חגים listed exactly as in 2 Chron. 8:13. Secondary insertions in Deut. 16:1-8 (i.e., vv. 3aβ, 4, 8),[26] however, associate the feast of Unleavened Bread with Passover, an association not found in Ex. 23 or 34 or in 2 Chron. 8:13, but explicit in the later Lev. 23:5-6 (H) and Ex. 12:1-20 (P). Presumably the Chronicler, knowing the priestly combination of Passover and Unleavened Bread and finding the text of Deut. 16:1-8 with the secondary references to the feast of Unleavened Bread already interpolated, took their combination for granted.[27]

In sum, then, it seems apparent that the Chronicler in this text (2 Chron. 8:12-13) has added specificity to the general statement in his source (1 Kgs. 9:25). The details, as in previously discussed instances, indicate a knowledge of Num. 28-29. However, the

---

[25] Noth assigns this text to a special source, neither J nor E. Cf. Noth, *Exodus*, pp. 173-75.

[26] Gerhard von Rad, *Deuteronomy: A Commentary*, The Old Testament Library, trans. Dorothea Barton (London, 1966), pp. 112-13.

[27] Each of the Chronicler's descriptions of Passover includes Unleavened Bread (2 Chron. 30, 35; Ezra 6:19-22).

Chronicler has not adhered strictly to Num. 28-29, which requires five annual feasts, but has rather followed the Deuteronomic calendar (Deut. 16:1-16), which is limited to the three feasts identified at 2 Chron. 8:13. Why the Chronicler did this is not clear. Perhaps he was reluctant to add to the "three time a year" (1 Kgs. 9:25) of his source. In any case, what is important for our investigation is the apparent ease with which the Chronicler can combine late priestly and Deuteronomic legislation and the authority (מצות משה, 2 Chron. 8:13) he accords it.

Summary

In the preceding section we have considered several texts which describe aspects of the regular sacrificial ritual which are claimed to conform exactly to the torah of Yahweh, the commandment of Moses, or some similar formula. Our investigation of antecedent legislation (pentateuchal or otherwise) on which these descriptions might be based, and thus to which authority was accorded, has suggested repeatedly that the late priestly Num. 28-29 and Lev. 24:1-9 were in the Chronicler's view. We have seen in addition, however, that the annual set feasts are listed (2 Chron. 8:13) after D (Deut. 16:1-16) and not Num. 28-29 or Lev. 23. This fact argues in favor of the view that the Chronicler's Torah was more than the latest law code, that indeed it contained both Deuteronomic and late priestly instruction.

Sukkoth

As we have already seen, 2 Chron. 8:13 lists Sukkoth as one of the three annual feasts. It was in fact the major feast,[28] at least since exilic times, and is referred to elsewhere as "the feast which is in the seventh month" (2 Chron. 5:3) or simply "the feast" (Ezek. 45:25, 2 Chron. 7:8 and cf. 1 Kgs. 8:65). But while these names are late, the festival itself goes back to Israel's earliest days in Canaan and is included in each of the Hebrew Bible's cultic calendars.

In the Covenant Code (Ex. 23:16) and in J (Ex. 34:22) the feast is known as "Ingathering" (אסיף), and is clearly an agricultural festival associated with the autumnal harvest at year's end. As harvest time will have varied from year to year, no specific date is

---

[28] Noth, *Leviticus*, p. 175.

set. Neither for that matter is any instruction given as to the length
or manner of its celebration. There is, in fact, no mention at all of
the סכה.

From the Deuteronomic calendar (Deut. 16:13-15) we learn
that the feast, now referred to as חג הסכה (Deut. 16:13, 16), is to be
kept joyfully for seven days. The date remains flexible, "when you
make your ingathering (באספך) from your threshing floor and your
wine press" (Deut. 16:13), but the place, in keeping with the
Deuteronomic program, is now specified: "the place which the Lord
will choose" (Deut. 16:15). The Deuteronomistic Historian, in a
passage supplementary to Deuteronomy (31:9-13),[29] adds the
requirement that the Torah be read by the priests to all Israel at
sabbatical year celebrations of Sukkoth.

Considerably more detail is provided by Lev. 23, which in its
original form belonged to the Holiness Code. The chapter has
clearly experienced substantial redaction. It has two introductions
(vv. 2 and 4), two conclusions (vv. 37-38 and 44) and two
descriptions of the Sukkoth ritual (vv. 33-36 and 39-43), the second
of which seems itself to have been further expanded, as we shall
see.[30]

In the basic stratum of the Holiness Code (Lev. 23:33-36), in
keeping with Deuteronomy 16:13-15, the festival is termed הסכות
חג, but it is now dated specifically to the fifteenth day of the seventh
month. Moreover, in addition to the seven days of the feast proper,
for the first time mention is made of an eighth day עצרת (v. 36).
The later vv. 39-43 is itself composite as the conclusion at v. 41
shows.[31] Verse 40 contains the earliest extant instructions on the
gathering of fruit and branches, but makes no mention of the סכה.
Indeed, since it includes gathering fruit and is associated with the
commandment to rejoice before the Lord, it seems more likely to be
related to the procession with the citron and palm fronds, than to the
material out of which to build the booths.[32] Following the
concluding statements of v. 41, the addition in vv. 42-43 provides

[29] Noth, *Überlieferungsgeschichtliche Studien I*, p. 39; von Rad, *Deuteronomy*, p. 188.

[30] de Vaux, *Ancient Israel*, pp. 472-73; Noth, *Leviticus*, pp. 166, 175-76.

[31] Noth, *Leviticus*, pp. 175-76.

[32] de Vaux, *Ancient Israel*, pp. 497-98; Noth, *Leviticus*, p. 175; Rudolph, *Esra und Nehemia*, p. 151. De Vaux dates the addition of vv. 42-43 prior to the addition of vv. 40-41 (p. 497), but v. 41 is then a superfluous conclusion. Noth (p. 175) rightly reverses the order of these additions.

the first (and only biblical) command to live in booths for the seven days duration of the feast proper[33] and an explanation of the practice derived from Israel's history.

The treatment of Sukkoth in the program of Ezekiel is remarkably brief (Ezek. 45:25). The feast is to be celebrated on the fifteenth day of the seventh month and for the seven days following (no mention is made of an eighth day), on each of which prescribed offerings, identical to those for the seven days of Unleavened Bread (cf. Ezek. 45:23-25), are to be made. Nothing is said of gathering fruit or branches, rejoicing before the Lord, or living in booths. That need not, however, be taken to indicate that such practices were unknown or rejected by Ezekiel. His treatment of Sukkoth is governed by his concern to detail precisely the prince's obligation to provide the material for all the regular required sacrifices (Ezek. 45:17, 23, 25).

The lengthiest instruction for Sukkoth is contained in the Pentateuch's latest ritual calendar, Num. 28-29. This instruction (Num. 29:12-38), however, consists almost entirely of a day-by-day enumeration of the required animal, cereal and drink offerings במספרם כמשפט (by number, according to ordinance).[34] Nothing is said of gathering branches or living in booths; the feast is not even named. It is simply a feast on the fifteenth day of the seventh month which is to last seven days (Num. 29:12) plus an eighth (Num. 29:35-38) during which time a very large quantity of animals is to be sacrificed along with cereal and drink offerings.

If we turn to consider the Chronicler's statements about Sukkoth, and compare them with the ritual instructions from the various codes reviewed above, we should be able to discover both the degree to which his views are based on antecedent legislation and which code (or codes) in each instance functions as his authority. The relevant texts are 2 Chron. 7:8-10, Ezra 3:4 and Neh. 8:13-18.[35]

---

[33] Although this must have been an ancient custom. Cf. Noth, *Leviticus*, pp. 175-76.

[34] The phrase occurs seven times (Num. 29:18, 21, 24, 27, 30, 37, and the variant at v. 33) with reference to these Sukkoth offerings. The ordinance cited is not a part of any extant biblical legislation.

[35] The feast is also mentioned in 2 Chron. 5:3 and 8:13. The former dates it in the seventh month, and the latter includes it as one of the three annual feasts. There is nothing in either text to indicate the Chronicler's authorities.

2 Chronicles 7:8-10
While the Chronicler in this text describing the Sukkoth of Solomon makes no claim that the ritual was according to the law, his careful modifications of his source (1 Kgs. 8:65) make clear the fact that he has firm convictions regarding the proper conduct of the feast. These convictions, based no doubt on the practice of his own day and written anachronistically into this ancient celebration, are authorized by texts which the Chronicler takes to be authoritative and which can be identified.

According to 1 Kgs. 8 Solomon dedicated the temple and kept Sukkoth (החג) in the seventh month (v. 2). The feast described in vv. 65-66 conforms exactly to the Deuteronomic torah (Deut. 16:13-15) in that it was a seven day feast held in Jerusalem to which all the people had rallied.[36]   On the eighth day, the feast having been completed, the people were dismissed and sent to their homes. The Chronicler preserved this event in his narrative, but has modified it to the extent that it no longer conforms to the requirements of Deuteronomy. To be sure, the feast is still kept in Jerusalem for seven days (2 Chron. 7:8), but on the eighth day the people are not dismissed. Instead, in conformity with the Holiness Code (Lev. 23:36, 39) and the later Num. 29:35, a "solemn assembly" (עצרת) was held. The people were dismissed on the following day, that is on the twenty-third day of the seventh month (v. 10), which dates the feast exactly. The dedication of the altar was kept from the eighth to the fourteenth, Sukkoth from the fifteenth to the twenty-second (eight days including the עצרת) and the people were dismissed on the twenty-third day of the seventh month.[37]   This implicit date, too, is a modification of 1 Kgs. 8:65-66, which like Deut. 16:13-15 is vague about the specific date of the feast. Here too the Chronicler is following the torah of Lev. 23:34, 39 and Num. 29:12.[38]

For our purposes, this text in the Chronicler's History is particularly helpful. His conscious, careful alteration of his source

---

[36] The gloss at 1 Kgs. 8:65 adding a second seven-day feast is probably due to the influence of the Chronicler's account (2 Chron. 7:8-10) in which the dedication of the altar lasted seven days and was followed by the seven-day feast of Sukkoth. See Ackroyd, *1 and 2 Chronicles, Ezra, Nehemiah*, p. 115.

[37] Rudolph, *Chronikbücher*, p. 217.

[38] Ezekiel 45:25 also dates the feast from the fifteenth to the twenty-first, but as noted above it lacks the eighth day assembly.

(which was authorized by D) demonstrates clearly the Chronicler's preference, in this instance, for the later priestly torah.

Ezra 3:4
This brief statement parallels the text just considered (2 Chron. 7:8-10). There, having built and dedicated the altar, Solomon together with "all Israel" kept Sukkoth. In Ezra 3:1-4, having rebuilt the altar but prior even to relaying the foundations of the temple (v. 6), Jeshua and Zerubbabel are said to have restored the sacrificial ritual ככתוב בתורת משה and to have kept Sukkoth ככתוב (v. 4). Keeping Sukkoth "as it is written" included, at least in part, the offering of burnt sacrifices "by number according to the ordinance, as each day required" (v. 4). The phrase, במספר כמשפט, used here and at 1 Chron. 23:31 by the Chronicler, occurs elsewhere in the Hebrew Bible only in Num. 29, where, as we have noted above, it is used seven times in reference to the daily Sukkoth offerings.[39]   In Ezra 3:4 too, therefore, it seems probable that the Chronicler is following the late priestly torah of Num. 28-29, and that it is to that text that he refers when he writes ככתוב.

Nehemiah 8:13-18
From a literary-critical point of view Neh. 7:72b-9:37 is fraught with problems.[40]   In terms of content it is the continuation of the Ezra Narrative in Ezra 7-10.[41]

Throughout Neh. 8-9 (so also Ezra 7 and 10) Ezra is referred to in the third person, and most commentators have found pervasive evidence in this text of the Chronicler's own style.[42]   While Mowinckel maintains that the third person references are original and evidence that Ezra did not himself author the Ezra story,[43] the view adopted here is that of Eissfeldt, namely: "the Chronicler did actually extract the substance of Neh. 8-9 from the Ezra Memoirs,

---

[39] Cf. n. 34.

[40] Cf. the discussion in Myers, *Ezra. Nehemiah*, p. 152.

[41] Ackroyd, *1 and 2 Chronicles, Ezra, Nehemiah*, pp. 256, 293.

[42] Noth, *Überlieferungsgeschichtliche Studien I*, p. 128, regards the Chronicler as the author of the Ezra Narrative in Neh. 8-10.

[43] Sigmund Mowinckel, *Studien zu dem Buche Ezra--Nehemia III: Die Ezrageschichte und das Gesetz Moses* (Oslo, 1965), pp. 94-96.

but himself gave it its present form...and in doing so substituted for the first person reference to Ezra, the third person form."[44]

If Eissfeldt's view is correct then our text (Neh. 8:13-18) should be treated as the Chronicler's rewrite of an episode originally related in Ezra's Memoir. On the basis of Neh. 8:14, 17, however, Batten argues that the Chronicler cannot have authored this narrative. His argument is that the text assumes that the people knew nothing of Sukkoth until they made a study of Ezra's law. But according to Ezra 3:4 the feast had been kept in the post-exilic period. Since the Chronicler "would not have been guilty of such a stupid blunder as to contradict Ezra 3:4" it follows that he is not responsible for this text.[45]

For all its apparent plausibility, this argument breaks down on closer examination. In the first place, it is not clear that v. 17 is meant to claim that the feast had not been kept since the period of Joshua as Batten assumes.[46] On the contrary, Rudolph has argued forcefully that the new thing was not keeping Sukkoth or even living in booths but reading the law throughout the feast as stipulated by Deut. 31:10-11.[47] Secondly, it is not unlike the Chronicler to exaggerate his claims. An instructive example is found in his description of Josiah's Passover, which, ignoring his own account of the Passover of Hezekiah (2 Chron. 30), the Chronicler claims to have been the first since the days of Samuel (2 Chron. 35:18).

The foregoing discussion has not resolved the numerous literary difficulties of Neh. 8-9 and its relationship to the Ezra Memoir. Nevertheless it has indicated the grounds on which, at least provisionally, the description of Sukkoth in Neh. 8:13-18 will be taken to reflect the point of view of the Chronicler.

According to the text as we have it Ezra read "from" the law (Neh. 8:3) on the first day of the seventh month (v. 2). On the second day (v. 13) of the seventh month (as the context makes clear) certain clan leaders, priests and Levites joined Ezra to study the law, in which they read a command to live in booths during Sukkoth. They then sent the people out to the hills to collect branches with

---

44 Eissfeldt, *The Old Testament*, p. 548.

45 Batten, *The Books of Ezra and Nehemiah*, p. 363.

46 Batten, *The Books of Ezra and Nehemiah*, p. 362.

47 Rudolph, *Esra und Nehemia*, pp. 151-53. Williamson, *Israel*, p. 27, assumes the new thing to be living in huts.

which to make the booths.[48]   The people then kept the feast with joy for seven days followed by a solemn assembly on the eighth. Throughout the feast, as we have noted above, the law was read.

All this was based on a study of "the law" (v. 13), or as it is referred to elsewhere in the immediate context: "the book of the law of Moses which the Lord had given to Israel" (v. 1), "the book of the law" (v. 3), "the law of God" (v. 8), "the law that the Lord had commanded by Moses" (v. 14) and "the book of the law of God" (v. 18). Moreover, certain aspects of the ritual were done (or were to be done) "as it is written" (v. 15) or "according to the ordinance" (v. 18). Our question, of course, is to exactly what text(s) do these phrases refer.

According to v. 14 the command to live in booths during Sukkoth was found "written in the law." Now, although this practice surely goes back to Israel's early days in Canaan,[49] we have noted previously that the only extant text which actually prescribes dwelling in booths for the duration of the feast is Lev. 23:42, which is a late text, an addition to an addition to the Holiness Code.[50]

Verse 15 is the proclamation issued to the people:[51]   they are to collect branches to make booths "as it is written." The only pentateuchal text which requires the collection of branches at Sukkoth is Lev. 23:40. This fact misled Batten, who declared, "this story is based on the Lev. code...where the making of booths is required."[52]   As Rudolph pointed out, however, Lev. 23:40 does not indicate that the branches are to be collected for the purpose of making booths.[53]   Indeed, as we have already seen, the text requires the collection of fruit as well as branches and probably refers to the *Lulab*.[54]   The fact that Neh. 8:13-18 makes no mention

---

[48] Verse 15 is a proclamation given by the leaders to the people and is not a part of what was found written in the law. Batten, *The Books of Ezra and Nehemiah*, p. 361; Myers, *Ezra. Nehemiah*, p. 155; Ackroyd, *1 and 2 Chronicles, Ezra, Nehemiah*, p. 297; Rudolph, *Esra und Nehemia*, p. 150.

[49] de Vaux, *Ancient Israel*, p. 497; Noth, *Leviticus*, p. 176.

[50] Cf. pp. 97-98.

[51] Cf. n. 48.

[52] Batten, *The Books of Ezra and Nehemiah*, p. 361.

[53] Rudolph, *Esra und Nehemia*, p. 151.

[54] Cf. p. 97.

of the collecting of fruit is further evidence that ככתוב (v. 15) does not refer to Lev. 23:40.

Since no other text in the Hebrew Bible even contains the command to collect branches, let alone with the stated purpose of building booths, we must conclude that if the Chronicler had a specific text in mind as his authority, that text is no longer extant. But that is to suggest that the Pentateuch had not yet attained its fixed form and canonical status. The Chronicler may have carelessly attributed to the Torah book what he thought was there but in fact was not; but if he referred to a text which did not get included in the final form of the Pentateuch, or claimed the authority of the written Torah for an instruction he knew it did not contain, thus in effect writing new instruction, then it would follow that the contents of the Pentateuch had not yet been fixed.

The Chronicler goes on to note that the feast was kept for seven days after which, on the eighth day, a solemn assembly (עצרת) was held כמשפט (v. 18). This parallels the Chronicler's statement at 2 Chron. 7:9, and like the latter conforms to Lev. 23:36, 39 and Num. 29:35. The daily reading from Torah, on the other hand, while not specifically identified as a requirement of Ezra's law, recalls the stipulation of the Deuteronomistic Historian that Torah be read as a part of the Sukkoth ritual on sabbatical years (Deut. 31:10-11).

Finally, although our text (Neh. 8:13-18) does not state the exact dates in the seventh month on which the feast was kept, there is no reason to doubt that in this respect too the Chronicler has followed priestly torah and intends that the reader assume it was held from the fifteenth through the twenty-second day (Lev. 23:33, 39; Num. 29:12; cf. 2 Chron. 7:8-10). As de Vaux has pointed out, the thirteen days from the reading of the law on the second (Neh. 8:13) to the beginning of Sukkoth on the fifteenth day of the seventh month would be required to assemble the people at Jerusalem and to prepare for the feast.[55]

Summary
In this section I have examined the Chronicler's three descriptions of Sukkoth. The investigation has shown that the Chronicler's accounts conform almost entirely to the requirements of late priestly torah, primarily Lev. 23:33-36, 42 but also Num.

---

[55] de Vaux, *Ancient Israel*, p. 500; Batten, *The Books of Ezra and Nehemiah*, p. 361.

29:12-38. We have noted in addition, in the discussion of Neh. 8:18, a possible relationship to Deut. 31:10-11. The Chronicler thus seems to know and to regard as authoritative the full range of pentateuchal legislation concerning Sukkoth. Neh. 8:15, however, has been shown to suggest that the final delimitation of the Pentateuch had by the time of the Chronicler, not yet occurred.

Passover and Unleavened Bread

The present books of Chronicles, Ezra, and Nehemiah describe three celebrations of the feast of Passover and Unleavened Bread. The people kept the feast as a part of Hezekiah's reform following the repair and rededication of the temple (2 Chron. 30:1-27), as a part of the reforms of Josiah, again following the repair of the temple (2 Chron. 35:1-19), and finally as a part of the post-exilic restoration of the cult in Jerusalem immediately following the dedication of the second temple (Ezra 6:19-22).

The descriptions of the feasts of Hezekiah and Josiah include a number of details on the exact manner in which the feast was kept. Moreover, at several points in these narratives the Chronicler notes explicitly that certain of these details conformed to the written law.[56] Clearly the Chronicler believed that the correct ritual for Passover and Unleavened Bread was based on authoritative texts. But which ones? Many scholars, following Wellhausen, have found the influence of P pervasive in the Chronicler's History. Roland de Vaux, a representative of this view, argued that the Chronicler's descriptions of the feast are in accord with P and not Deuteronomy.[57] Gerhard von Rad, on the other hand, argued at length that the Chronicler was influenced at least as much by Deuteronomy as by P,[58] and specifically that the Chronicler's descriptions of Passover and Unleavened Bread depend almost entirely on Deuteronomy.[59] My analysis of the texts in question yields somewhat more complex results.

---

[56] "As it is written" (ככתוב) occurs at 2 Chron. 30:5, 18; 35:12. Cf. 2 Chron. 30:16; 35:6, 13.

[57] de Vaux, *Ancient Israel*, p. 487.

[58] Gerhard von Rad, *Das Geschichtsbild des Chronistischen Werkes* (Stuttgart, 1930), pp. 38-63.

[59] von Rad, *Geschichtsbild*, pp. 52-53.

I will begin by describing the canonical stipulations for Passover and the feast of Unleavened Bread as they are found in the various pentateuchal law codes and Ezekiel. I will then examine the Chronicler's three accounts of the feast. A comparison of these accounts with pentateuchal legislation will show that some of the details of the Chronicler's accounts of Passover and Unleavened Bread conform to the requirements of P, some to D, and others to one of the other pentateuchal legal collections. Some of the details, however, appear to reflect the program of Ezekiel, and others, although attributed to the book or law of Moses, have no antecedent basis in the Hebrew Bible.

Israel's Early Traditions

Israel's earliest religious calendars, Ex. 23:14-17 and Ex. 34:18-23, both describe the feast of Unleavened Bread (חג המצות), but neither refers to Passover.[60] The Yahwist's instructions for Passover (Ex. 12:21-23, 27b, 39) are likewise ancient, but make no mention of the feast of Unleavened Bread.[61]

According to Ex. 23:15, the feast of Unleavened Bread was one of the three annual pilgrimage feasts kept to Yahweh. The verse has probably been expanded at the end, but in its original form it stipulated a seven-day feast in the month of Abib during which unleavened bread was to be eaten.[62] Exodus 34:18, likewise expanded, provides the same instruction, but nothing further.[63]

Passover is not included in these early calendars for two reasons. In the first place, the three annual feasts were Canaanite agricultural feasts which Israel adopted and then kept to Yahweh,[64]

[60] de Vaux, *Ancient Israel*, pp. 471, 486. Ex. 34:25 refers to Passover and terms it a "pilgrimage feast" (חג), probably influenced by the reference to a חג in the parallel Lev. 23:18 (which, however, does not refer to Passover). Since Passover is not identified as a חג until Deuteronomy, the editing of these texts must be later than D. Cf. Noth, *Exodus*, pp. 190-92, 264-65.

[61] But cf. v. 39 which mentions the quickly made "unleavened cakes" (מצות).

[62] Noth, *Exodus*, p. 190. The date is not specified because the feast was originally tied to the harvest, which would vary from year to year. de Vaux, *Ancient Israel*, p. 471.

[63] Noth, *Exodus*, p. 265.

[64] Noth, *Exodus*, pp. 190-91; de Vaux, *Ancient Israel*, p. 471.

while Passover had a different origin.[65]   And secondly, as the J
account of the Passover ritual (Ex. 12:21-23, 27b) makes clear,
Passover, at least after the settlement in Canaan, was not a
pilgrimage feast but a family celebration, only later joined to the
feast of Unleavened Bread.[66]

The Yahwist (Ex. 12:21-23, 27b, 39), on the other hand, does
not mention the feast of Unleavened Bread, but does provide
detailed instructions for keeping the Passover. The elders of the
community must select a lamb or kid (צאן) for their respective
families. Each elder then kills the Passover victim (שחט הפסח) for
his family and dabs its blood around the doorway of the house in
which the family observes the Passover. If the Yahwist originally
included a date for this meal, it was lost in the editorial process of
incorporating J's instructions for the Passover into the P narrative of
Ex. 12.

Deuteronomy
The religious calendar of Deuteronomy (16:1-17) in its section
on Passover and the feast of Unleavened Bread (vv. 1-8) introduces
a number of important changes and additions to the required ritual.
The most important of these is its transformation of the formerly
familial Passover celebration into a pilgrimage feast. Passover is no
longer to be celebrated "within any of your towns . . . but at the
place which the Lord your God will choose" (Deut. 16:5-6.). The
people must assemble in Jerusalem for Passover and return to their
homes *the next morning* (v. 7). The requirements for the seven-day
feast of Unleavened Bread, the people already having returned home
from the pilgrimage, are clearly secondary.[67]

As a consequence of this centralization of the celebration,
Passover becomes a part of the temple's sacrificial ritual. The
people no longer simply kill (שחט, cf. Ex. 12:21, J) the Passover
victim, they now sacrifice (זבה, Deut, 16:2, 5) it.[68] The people
may now sacrifice an ox as well as a lamb or kid (v. 2, צאן ובקר),

---

[65] Cf. de Vaux, *Ancient Israel*, pp. 488-90; J. B. Segal, *The Hebrew Passover:
From the Earliest Times to A.D. 70*, (London, 1963), pp. 78-113.

[66] de Vaux, *Ancient Israel*, p. 488; Noth, *Exodus*, p. 191.

[67] As are 3aβ, 4. von Rad, *Deuteronomy*, pp. 112-13; de Vaux, *Ancient Israel*,
pp. 485-86. Note also that the deuteronomistic account of the Passover of
Josiah (2 Kgs. 23:21-23) indicates that it was a pilgrimage feast kept in
Jerusalem, and that it too lacks any reference to the feast of Unleavened Bread.

[68] זבה is used in Ex. 34:25, but is an addition to J based on D. Cf. n. 60.

but in any case they must boil (בשׁל, v. 7) it. Finally, as in former times, Passover occurs on the evening of an unspecified day in the month of Abib (vv. 1, 6).

The Holiness Code

The religious calendar of the Holiness Code (Lev. 23) reflects two major developments in the manner of keeping Passover and the feast of Unleavened Bread. In the first place, the two are now clearly associated; and secondly, both are precisely fixed in the liturgical calendar (Lev. 23:5-8). Passover takes place on the fourteenth day of the seventh month and is followed by the seven day feast of Unleavened Bread. The text says nothing more about Passover, but emphasizes instead the ritual of the feast of Unleavened Bread. For seven days the people must eat unleavened bread (v. 6). On the first and seventh day they may do no work; it is a holy convocation (מקרא־קדשׁ, vv. 7-8). Finally, fire offerings (אשׁה) are to be presented (קרב) on each of the seven days of the feast (v. 8).

Ezekiel

Passover and the feast of Unleavened Bread are first associated in the Holiness Code; in Ezek. 45:21-24 they are for the first time viewed as one feast (חג, v. 21). As in Lev. 23 the feast begins on the fourteenth day of the first month; the people must eat unleavened bread for seven days during which time the prince must also arrange for required daily animal sacrifices. Ezekiel does not mention a holy convocation (מקרא־קדשׁ) on the first and last day of the feast, but, unlike the Holiness Code, does specify the required sacrifices. On the fourteenth of the month the people offer a bull (פר) as a sin offering (חטאת) and on each of the following seven days they sacrifice seven bulls and seven lambs (אילים) as a burnt offering (עולה) as well as one goat (עז) as a sin offering. In addition, they must make cereal and oil offerings in specific measure. Finally, although unparalleled in Israel's codes of law, Ezekiel requires the prince (נשׂיא) to provide all the animals, cereal and oil for these sacrifices.[69]

---

[69] The people contribute to the prince, who then apportions the material as the ritual requires (Ezek. 45:13-16).

The Priestly Code

Our survey of biblical texts which describe the requirements for observing Passover and the feast of Unleavened Bread has to this point revealed a progressive development. The two celebrations have been brought together, dated precisely, and made a part of the central sacrificial cult. In addition, a number of details specifying the source, kind, number, and manner of the sacrifices have been added. The Priestly Code's treatment of Passover and Unleavened Bread (Ex. 12:1-20) does not, however, continue on this trajectory. Instead, on major issues P rejects Deuteronomic and subsequent stipulations in favor of earlier practices.

The most obvious and important of these changes is that P completely removes Passover and Unleavened Bread from the temple cult. Gone are all references to burnt offerings and sacrifices, including even the fire offerings (אשה) of H (Lev. 23:8). The lamb or kid, no longer sacrificed as in Deuteronomy (16:2, 5, 6), is now simply killed (שחט, v. 6) as in J (Ex. 12:21). This takes place not in Jerusalem (cf. Deut. 16:5-7) but in each private home (vv. 5-7). As in J (Ex. 12:22) blood is smeared on the doorway (v. 7). In a direct correction of Deut. 16:7, P (Ex. 12:8-9) stipulates that the lamb or kid be roasted with fire (צלי־אש) and not boiled in water (בשל מבשל במים).[70] Finally, the animal is to be eaten in haste with unleavened bread and bitter herbs in memory of the exodus; what is uneaten must be burned (vv. 8, 10-11, 14).

P has not, however, changed every detail. Passover is still closely joined to the feast of Unleavened Bread.[71] The dates remain the same (Ex. 12:18), and like the Holiness Code (Lev. 23:7), but unlike Ezekiel, P stipulates that Unleavened Bread begin and end with a holy convocation (מקרא־קדש, Ex. 12:16).

There are also certain refinements. According to P the selection of the passover animal must take place on the tenth day of the first month (v. 3), and the animal itself must be an unblemished

---

[70] von Rad, *Deuteronomy,* p. 112, suggests that the Deuteronomic requirement of boiling the meat "probably corresponds to the custom at the sanctuaries where the meat to be eaten by the worshipping congregation was boiled in large cauldrons (1 Sam. 2:12ff.)." If this is correct the requirement that it be roasted and not boiled may be a part of P's decentralization of the Passover.

[71] It is difficult, however, to imagine Israel having a peaceful seven day feast of Unleavened Bread following the night of the Passover in Egypt. Cf. Noth, *Exodus,* p. 97.

one year old male from the flock (שה, vv. 3, 4, 5), either a lamb or a kid (עז, כבש v. 5).

Numbers 28:16-25

No trace of P's revision remains in Num. 28:16-25, the latest stratum of pentateuchal legislation for Passover and the feast of Unleavened Bread. In fact, nothing is said of Passover itself except that it is on the fourteenth day of the first month. While this is also the date in P (Ex. 12:6, 18), it is clear from the virtual identity of Num. 28:16-19a, 25 and Lev. 23:5-8 (H) that this late text depends on H rather than the priestly Ex. 12:1-20. Thus, like Lev. 23:5-8, our text stipulates that Passover is on the fourteenth day of the seventh month and is followed by the seven-day feast of Unleavened Bread, the first and seventh day of which are marked by their mandatory holy convocation (מקרא־קדש, vv. 16, 17, 25). Moreover, like H (Lev. 23:8) but unlike P, daily offerings by fire (אשה) are to be made for the duration of the feast. Numbers 28:16-25 goes beyond H, however, at this point, and in doing so is reminiscent of Ezek. 45:21-24. That is, the required daily offering by fire (אשה, Lev. 23:8, Num. 28:19) is further identified as a burnt offering (עולה) the contents of which are exactly specified: two young bulls, one ram and seven male lambs a year old together with specified amounts of flour and oil for a cereal offering, and one male goat for a sin offering (vv. 19-24). As we have seen, Ezek. 45:23-24 requires a very similar burnt offering (עולה) on each of the feast's seven days.

Passover and Unleavened Bread
in the Chronicler's History

Having reviewed all of ancient Israel's canonical legislation for Passover and the feast of Unleavened Bread, I turn now to the Chronicler's three narrative accounts of the feast. As we will see, the Chronicler claims at a number of points that various details of the ritual were performed "as it is written" (ככתוב), "according to the Torah of Moses" (כתורת משה), "according to the word of Yahweh by Moses" (כדבר־יהוה ביד משה), "according to the ordinance" (כמשפט), or "as it is written in the book of Moses" (בספר משה ככתוב).[72]   A comparison of these details with the requirements of

---

[72] 2 Chron. 30:5, 16, 18; 35:6, 12, 13.

the legislation surveyed above will demonstrate the Chronicler's complex and eclectic use of Israelite legal tradition. Although he regards legislation from each of the Pentateuch's legal collections as authoritative, his book of law is neither the Pentateuch nor any of its sources.

The Passover of Hezekiah: 2 Chronicles 30:1-27

The Chronicler's first and longest narrative of a feast of Passover and Unleavened Bread is not derived from 2 Kings. It is widely regarded to be the Chronicler's own composition, although it may have been based on a description of Unleavened Bread which can no longer be recovered.[73]   In what follows, I will examine the specific details of how the feast was celebrated and describe their relationships to antecedent Israelite law.

1) The place where Passover and Unleavened Bread was kept.

2 Chron. 30:1, 3, 5, and 13 stress the requirement that all Israel should assemble in Jerusalem for the feast of Passover and Unleavened Bread. Verse 5 goes so far as to note that the people "had not kept it in great numbers as prescribed" (ככתוב).[74]   The Chronicler, it appears, knows a text which he takes to be the authority on the basis of which Passover is held in Jerusalem. One thinks immediately of Deut. 16:1-8, the first text to state such a requirement,[75]   but Ezek. 45:21-24, Num. 28:16-25, and the

---

[73] Scholars differ on the question of the event's historicity. Curtis and Madsen, *Chronicles*, p. 471, and de Vaux, *Ancient Israel*, p. 487, view it as a product of the Chronicler's imagination, while Myers, *II Chronicles*, p. 178, thinks the Chronicler's story is not wholly invented. Williamson, *1 and 2 Chronicles*, pp. 360-65, reviews the issues and argues that Hezekiah did in fact celebrate Unleavened Bread in the second month (but not Passover as it was not joined to Unleavened Bread until the time of Josiah), and that the Chronicler had an account of the event which he completely rewrote. Cf. Segal, *The Hebrew Passover*, pp. 228-30.

[74] Adam C. Welch, *The Work of the Chronicler: Its Purpose and Date* (London, 1939), pp. 133-35, assumes the "they" in this clause to refer exclusively to people from the north, who had not been able to keep Passover as prescribed (by Deut.) because their sanctuaries had been destroyed by Assyria. The verse itself, however, identifies the subject as the people of all Israel "from Beersheba to Dan," that is, Judeans and Israelites.

[75] von Rad, *Geschichtsbild*, p. 52, argues that the location of Passover in Jerusalem is the Chronicler's main point, that it derives from Deut. 16:1-8 and 2

Holiness Code (Lev. 23:5-8) all presuppose Jerusalem as the site of the daily burnt offerings of Unleavened Bread. What can be said with certainty is that the Chronicler is not following the stipulations of J (Ex. 12:21-27), nor is it the Priestly Code (Ex. 12:1-20) with its decentralized family celebration to which the Chronicler refers and on which his description depends.

2) The date of Passover and Unleavened Bread.
       According to 2 Chron. 30:15, Hezekiah's Passover was kept on the fourteenth day of the second month. But vv. 2-3 make clear that the normal practice was to keep the Passover on the fourteenth day of the first month, the month long delay having been necessitated by a lack of sanctified priests and the people's need for additional time to make their way to Jerusalem. As we have seen, from the Holiness Code (Lev. 23:5) on all of Israel's traditions set the fourteenth day of the first month as the date for Passover. The authorization to delay the Feast, however, may be found in Num. 9:6-11, a P text. There the question is put: What if a person is unclean or away on a journey at the appointed time for Passover? The answer provided by Yahweh is that such a person should celebrate the feast one month later, on the fourteenth day of the second month. Because the grounds for postponing the celebration in 2 Chron. 30:3 and Num. 9:10 are quite different, von Rad argued that the Chronicler was not following this P text.[76] There is some merit to this objection. For P Passover is celebrated at one's home so the reference to a journey (Num. 9:10) cannot refer to a pilgrimage to Jerusalem as 2 Chron. 30:3 would require. In addition the uncleanness in Num. 9:6-7 is corpse contamination while 2 Chron. 30:3 refers simply to "unsanctified priests."
       An alternative explanation is offered by Talmon, who argued that the delay was to accommodate people from the North whose calendar was a month behind that of the South.[77] While this is an attractive suggestion, the fact is that according to the Chronicler Passover could not have been kept in Jerusalem at the normal time because the temple was not sanctified until the sixteenth day of the first month (2 Chron. 29:17). Despite von Rad's arguments it

---

Kgs. 23, and that, therefore, the Chronicler is following D and rejecting P's *häusliches Fest*.

[76] von Rad, *Geschichtsbild*, p. 53.

[77] Shemaryahu Talmon, "Divergencies in Calendar Reckoning in Ephraim and Judah," *VT*, VIII (1958), 48-74. Cf. 1 Kgs. 12:32-33.

seems more likely that the text reflects the extent to which the Chronicler found room to interpret for his own day the spirit of Num. 9:6-11.[78]

3) The animal sacrifices of Passover and Unleavened Bread.

At Hezekiah's Passover the victim is termed הפסח (*RSV*: "the passover lamb"), and it is killed (שחט) not sacrificed (2 Chron. 30:15, 17). This phrase (שחט הפסח), which occurs in each of the Chronicler's Passover narratives,[79] occurs elsewhere only in Ex. 12:21 (J). According to P (Ex. 12:6) the victim is killed (שחט), but it is never referred to as הפסח; in Deut. 16:2, 5 the animal (never הפסח) is sacrificed (זבה).[80]

During the seven days of Unleavened Bread the people sacrificed peace offerings (זבהי שלמים) consisting of bulls (פרים) and sheep and goats (צאן vv. 22-24). According to Deut. 16:2 the Passover sacrifice could come from the flock (צאן) or the herd (בקר), but Deuteronomy makes no mention of sacrifices during Unleavened Bread. The Holiness Code (Lev. 23:8) mentions a daily offering by fire (אשה), but only Ezek. 45:21-24 and Num. 28:19-22 specify the sacrificial animals, namely: bulls, rams, and goats (פרים, אילים, and עזים) in Ezekiel; and bulls, rams, lambs (כבשים) and goats in Numbers. P does not even refer to sacrifices during Unleavened Bread, and yet the phrase used by the Chronicler for these sacrifices (זבחי שלמים), which is nowhere else in the Hebrew Bible associated with Unleavened Bread, is a favorite of the priestly writers.[81] It is also used to describe a part of the covenant ratification ritual (Ex. 24:5, JE) and the covenant renewal ceremonies at Shechem (Deut. 27:7) and Mt. Ebal (Josh. 8:31). Most significantly, however, according to 1 Kgs. 8:63 peace offerings (זבחי שלמים) were offered at Solomon's dedication of the temple. Although neither mentions this fact, both Myers and Williamson point out that the Chronicler's model for Hezekiah's Passover was Solomon's dedication of the temple.[82] Both were

---

[78] Ackroyd, *1 and 2 Chronicles, Ezra, Nehemiah*, p. 184.

[79] 2 Chron. 30:15, 17; 35:1, 6, 11; Ezra 6:20. The Passover victim is termed פסח elsewhere only in 2 Chron. 35:7, 8, 9, 13.

[80] von Rad, *Geschichtsbild*, p. 53, argues that the Chronicler basically follows the Deuteronomic Passover legislation, but allows that this is an exception.

[81] Brown, Driver and Briggs, *Lexicon*, p. 257b.

[82] Myers, *II Chronicles*, p. 179; Williamson, *Israel*, pp. 119-25.

kept for fourteen days rather than the required seven (2 Chron. 7:8-9; 30:23), but it was Sukkoth that followed the dedication of the temple and Passover which follows Hezekiah's rededication. The זבחי שלמים of Solomon's feast (1 Kgs. 8:63), simply השלמים in the Chronicler's account of that event (2 Chron. 7:7), appear to have been transferred to his account of Hezekiah's Passover (2 Chron. 30:22) for which he had no *Vorlage* in Kings. Thus it is likely that this phrase, although a characteristic of P, is present in our text due to the influence of 1 Kgs. 8:63 rather than the Priestly Code.

The source of the animals sacrificed as peace offerings is not as explicit as one could desire, but it seems likely that the meaning of v. 24 is that they were all provided by Hezekiah and the princes (השרים), presumably from their own possessions (cf. 2 Chron. 31:3). According to 1 Kgs. 8:63 (and 2 Chron. 7:5), at the dedication of the temple Solomon sacrificed peace offerings from the herd (בקר) and flock (צאן). The implication is that the animals belonged to him. Strangely, however, none of the pentateuchal texts which require sacrifices during the feast of Unleavened Bread indicate who is responsible for providing the animals. Only Ezekiel addresses this question. The people contribute them to the prince (הנשיא), who then provides them as they are required for the sacrificial ritual (Ezek. 45:15, 17, 21). While these instructions may have influenced the Chronicler, it seems likely that here again he is following the Solomonic precedent described in 1 Kings, which, unlike Ezekiel, says nothing about the people's contribution. For the Chronicler, Hezekiah's wealth, like Solomon's[83] is sufficient for him to provide "from his own possessions" (2 Chron. 31:3).

4) Official functions of priests and Levites.

According to 2 Chron. 30:13-15a, a large congregation (including a few people from the Northern Kingdom, v. 11) assembled in Jerusalem, removed unacceptable altars, and "killed the passover lamb" (*RSV*; MT: וישחטו הפסח). The zeal of these laymen put the priests and Levites to shame (v. 15b). They therefore sanctified themselves, brought burnt offerings into the temple and took their posts "according to the law of Moses" (משה כתורת v. 15b-16). The Levites then slew the paschal offering (הפסח שחטו) for those not ritually prepared, and the priests manipulated the blood (v. 16-17).

---

83 Williamson, *Israel*, p. 122; Williamson, *1 and 2 Chronicles*, p. 373.

Myers, following Rudolph, suggests that having the Levites slay the Passover sacrifice was probably a misunderstanding since the law (he cites Ex. 12:6 and Deut. 16:6) assigned that task to the heads of families.[84] I think it more likely that the Chronicler has not so much misunderstood the law as supplemented it. The Hebrew Bible has no instructions at all for Levitical or priestly participation in the Passover ritual.[85] The Chronicler's formulaic "according to the law of Moses" (כתורת משה) in v. 16 claims legal authority, but refers to no canonical text.[86]

The Passover of Josiah: 2 Chronicles 35:1-19

For his account of the Passover held in the eighteenth year of Josiah the Chronicler had at his disposal the deuteronomistic account of the same event (2 Kgs. 23:21-23), which stresses that in accordance with the newly discovered book Passover was kept in Jerusalem in a way unparalleled since the rise of the monarchy. But how exactly was this Passover different? The text is brief and provides little information about how the Feast was kept. It gives no specific date, says nothing about the role of priests or Levites, and provides no information about the kind or number of animal sacrifices. We are told only that the Passover was kept in Jerusalem in accordance with the book. But as I have noted above, the great innovation of the book, that is of Deuteronomy, is that it changed the nature of Passover from a familial meal to a pilgrimage feast. Thus it appears that the one detail provided by 2 Kgs. 23:21-23,

---

[84] Myers, *II Chronicles*, pp. 178-79; Rudolph, *Chronikbücher*, p. 301. It is understandable that P, with its familial Passover ritual, would not assign a role to priests or Levites, but with the centralized observance of Deut. one would expect the clergy to take over functions previously assigned to the heads of families. Deut. 16:6, in fact, contrary to Myers' assertion, is ambiguous in regard to who exactly makes the sacrifice. It does not mention the heads of families or the clergy, but stresses instead the place at which the Passover sacrifice is to be made.

[85] Ezek. 44:10-16 may be connected with this, however. It does not deal specifically with Passover, but does say that the Levites are to slay (שחט) the burnt offering (עלם) and sacrifice (זבח) of the people.

[86] "as it is written" (ככתוב) in v. 18 is similar. The context deals with people who are not ritually prepared (clean) for Passover. The Hebrew Bible does not include specific instruction on how to prepare oneself for Passover, but does recognize that uncleanness disqualifies one from participation (cf. Num. 9:6-13). A striking feature of the passage is that the written requirements of the law are suspended to allow the sincere, although unclean, to participate.

namely that it was kept in Jerusalem, is precisely the detail which made Josiah's Passover so extraordinary.[87]

The Chronicler reproduced in his own account all the information provided him by his *Vorlage*. Even the problematic statement that no such Passover had been previously kept during the entire period of the monarchy is included.[88]   Moreover, the command of Josiah in 2 Kgs. 23:21 to "keep the Passover as it is written in this book of the covenant," while not quoted, is essentially reproduced in 2 Chron. 35:1-19 not just once but three times. We find in v. 6 the command to the Levites to discharge their cultic obligations "according to the word of the Lord by Moses" (כדבר־יהוה ביד־משה); in v. 12 it is said that the burnt offerings were set apart to be offered "as it is written in the book of Moses" (משה ככתוב בספר), and in the following verse the Passover sacrifice is claimed to have been roasted "according to the ordinance" (כמשפט).

Thus in his expanded version of the Kings account of Josiah's Passover, the Chronicler describes an event which like Hezekiah's Passover was kept in Jerusalem in accordance with the Deuteronomic prescription. Unlike that of Hezekiah, however, it was kept on the fourteenth day of the first month, that is on the date first specified at Lev. 23:5 (H) and unchanged in subsequent cultic calendars. There is, however, no real discrepancy between the dates observed by Hezekiah and Josiah. As we have observed, the Passover of Hezekiah was postponed due to extraordinary circumstances and on the authority of a P text (Num. 9:9-12). Thus it appears that the Chronicler requires that in normal circumstances Passover be a pilgrimage feast (חג) observed in Jerusalem on the fourteenth day of the first month. As we have seen, the place of the celebration and its character as a חג derive from D (Deut. 16:5-6, cf. 2 Kgs. 23:23), while the date, never specified in D, reflects later priestly texts.

With regard to the sacrificial victims and the official cultic roles of priests and Levites, the Passover of Josiah again closely parallels that of Hezekiah. The same kinds of animals were provided by the king and his princes; the Levites "killed the passover lamb" (הפסח

---

[87] de Vaux, *Ancient Israel*, pp. 486-88.

[88] Rudolph, *Chronikbücher*, p. 329, identifies the role of the Levites in Josiah's Passover as the new thing. But while it is true that 2 Chron. 35 describes their activities in more detail than we find in 2 Chron. 30, the Levites had the principal role in Hezekiah's Passover. Cf. Welch, *The Work of the Chronicler*, p. 113.

116   Torah and the Chronicler's History

וישחטו), and the priests sprinkled the blood "as it is written in the book of Moses" (ככתוב בספר משה, vv. 11-12). We have noted in connection with Hezekiah's Passover that the Pentateuch, indeed, the Hebrew Bible, nowhere assigns these or any other functions in the Passover ritual to priests or Levites. In the case of Josiah's Passover it is further stated that "they (the Levites, apparently) set aside the burnt offerings" (v. 12), presumably parts of the paschal victims, for the laity to offer to Yahweh. As Rudolph pointed out, the Hebrew Bible says nothing about this ritual which the Chronicler attributes to the book of Moses.[89]   The practice may, however, reflect a development from Ezek. 45:21-24 and Num. 28:16-25, which, like the Chronicler, view Passover and Unleavened Bread as a single feast (חג), and require a daily burnt offering (עולה) for the seven days of the feast.

A second point not mentioned in connection with Hezekiah's Passover but noted in our present text (v. 13) is that the Passover victim was roasted (ויבשלו הפסח באש) according to the ordinance (כמשפט). Myers translates the phrase as "boil in the fire" and finds here "a conflation of Ex. 12:8-9 (P), which requires roasting, and Deut. 16:7, which requires boiling."[90]   If this is true it provides important further evidence that the Chronicler regarded both D and P as authoritative and thus attempted to reconcile their differences. The text, however, may not be such a conflation.   The Deuteronomic stipulation is that the victim be boiled (בשל, Deut. 16:7), while P (Ex. 12:8-9) requires that it be roasted (צלי-אש) and not boiled (בשל במים). The contrast is between cooking in water and cooking[91] in fire, and in this instance the Chronicler follows P.[92]

The Passover of the Restoration Community: Ezra 6:19-22
This brief account describes a feast of Passover and Unleavened Bread very similar to those of Hezekiah (2 Chron. 30:1-27) and Josiah (2 Chron. 35:1-19). Even the context is the same:

---

[89] Rudolph, *Chronikbücher*, p. 327. The Chronicler, he believes, has been influenced by Lev. 3:6-16.

[90] Myers, *II Chronicles*, p. 211. So also Williamson, *1 and 2 Chronicles*, p. 407.

[91] בשל many times simply means "cook" (cf. Brown, Driver, and Briggs, *Lexicon*, p. 143a.

[92] Even von Rad, whose thesis is that the Chronicler has essentially based his descriptions on D, recognized that in this instance we have a deviation from D which conforms to P (cf. *Geschichtsbild*, p. 53).

After the dedication of the (second) temple, Passover and Unleavened Bread was celebrated, as in the former instances, in Jerusalem on the fourteenth day of the first month.[93] Once again the Levites killed the Passover victim (וישחטו הפסח) and the feast of Unleavened Bread was celebrated for seven days. We note, however, that the Chronicler has in the present case omitted any reference to the authority which warrants the cultic activities which he narrates.

The text is nevertheless of considerable significance. By paralleling the accounts of the Passovers of Hezekiah and Josiah it confirms our view that the Chronicler has in his mind, whether based on the practice of his own day or accurate historical sources, a single coherent notion of how Passover and Unleavened Bread was celebrated in accordance with the law. We have shown already that this notion and the laws to which it resorts for its authority are eclectic. It does not depend exclusively on D or P, but draws in varying degrees from the various legal collections of the Pentateuch. What then precludes the conclusion that the Chronicler therefore knew the Pentateuch as canonical authority? Just this: the practice of Passover as recorded by the Chronicler and attributed to the written Torah is not based exclusively on the Pentateuch either. The ritual functions of the priests and Levites, so important to the Chronicler and attributed by him to the law of Moses in 2 Chron. 30:16 and to the book of Moses in 2 Chron. 35:12 have no antecedent legislative basis in the Pentateuch.

Official Functions of Cultic Personnel

As we have just seen the Chronicler's claim that certain liturgical functions of the priests and Levites were in accordance with the law is not supported by any pentateuchal text. In fact the Chronicler frequently identifies David, and not Moses or the law, as the authority undergirding the official functions of the various cultic personnel. Thus the duties of the singers and gatekeepers and the divisions of the priests and Levites were all, so he claimed, established by David.[94] Lest one conclude from this that the

---

[93] Hezekiah's Passover was an exception, but the context makes clear that the normal date was the fourteenth day of the first month. See above, pp. 111-12.

[94] Cf. e.g., 1 Chron. 15:16, 27; 24:3; 25:1-3; 2 Chron. 8:14; 23:18; 29:26-28; Ezra 3:10; Neh. 12:45-46.

Chronicler was aware of what was and what was not required by the law of Moses, and that he therefore refrained from attributing to Moses what had not already been so attributed, [95] we note that at several places the organization of cultic personnel is in fact attributed to the book, or law, of Moses (2 Chron. 30:16; Ezra 6:18). Indeed, 2 Chron. 23:18 so entwines Davidic and Mosaic authority that one must conclude that for the Chronicler a distinction between what was required by David and what by Moses was non-existent--or at least not important.

On other points, however, pentateuchal texts do require certain activities of priests and Levites which the Chronicler describes, and for which he claims written authority. Thus in 1 Chron. 6:34 (Ev. 6:49) the offerings made by Aaron and his sons on the altar of burnt offering and the altar of incense are presented in accord with directives included in what is generally regarded as P (Ex. 27:1-8; 30:1-10). When the ark is brought to Jerusalem it is carried on the shoulders of Levites "as Moses had commanded" (1 Chron. 15:15, cf. 15:2). This too reflects priestly torah (Num. 4:4-15),[96] although an addition to Deuteronomy concurs in the assignment of this duty to the Levites (Deut. 10:8).[97] The *Vorlage* of 1 Chron. 15 (2 Sam. 6) makes no reference to Levites, and elsewhere the Deuteronomistic Historian states that priests brought the ark to the recently completed temple of Solomon (1 Kgs. 8:3). Not surprising is the Chronicler's correction: according to 2 Chron. 5:4 it was the Levites who carried the ark to the temple.[98]

The Nehemiah Memoir

The Nehemiah Memoir is being treated separately for several reasons, not the least of which is the fact that its relationship to pentateuchal legislation is unique among the constituent parts of the Chronicler's History Work. In the first place, although it describes

---

[95] This appears to be Eissfeldt's conclusion. Cf. Eissfeldt, *The Old Testament*, p. 549.

[96] An addition to P, according to Noth, *Exodus*, pp. 41-43.

[97] von Rad, *Deuteronomy*, pp. 79-80.

[98] The Chronicler concurs with his *Vorlage*, however, that it was the priests who took the ark into the inner sanctuary (2 Chron. 5:7; 1 Kgs. 8:6). In this, too, the Chronicler is following P (Num. 4:5-20). Cf. Rudolph, *Chronikbücher*, p. 209.

various offenses and reforms, as well as aspects of the establishment or regulation of social, economic and cultic practices and even a ceremony of dedication, it never claims the authority of the book of law. It does not, in any context, refer to the written authority which figures so prominently throughout the rest of the Chronicler's Work, nor in fact does the word תורה appear in the entire Memoir. Yet the reforms of Nehemiah are not unrelated to the legislation of the Pentateuch.

The closest the Memoir comes to a reference to the law is at Neh. 13:5 when the writer speaks of the tithes "which are given by commandment to the Levites, singers, and gatekeepers," and which as it turns out were not in fact being given to them (Neh. 13:10). The Deuteronomic law (Deut. 14:22-24) stipulates that the annual tithe be eaten by the people in celebration at the place the Lord chooses, but goes on to enjoin the people not to forget the Levite, and indeed prescribes that the tithes of every third year be shared by the Levite, the sojourner, the fatherless and the widow. The Priestly law on tithes (Num. 18:21-24), however, has closer affinities to Neh. 13:5-10. It is the only pentateuchal text to assign every tithe of the people of Israel to the Levites.

In Neh. 5:6-13 we have an account of Nehemiah's response to the complaint of the poor that they were losing their property and children to their creditors because they couldn't pay their debts to the wealthy in the community (Neh. 5:1-5). Nehemiah, we are told, thought the situation over and then publicly accused the leaders of charging interest and selling their brethren as slaves. The accused stood mute, and Nehemiah proceeded to order them to stop charging interest and to return to the poor the property they had extracted from them.

Although there is no reference to the law, Nehemiah's judgement against the practice of loaning at interest had strong legal grounds. As early as the Covenant Code Israelite law had prohibited the exacting of interest (Ex. 22:24, Ev. 22:25). The Deuteronomic law forbade interest on loans made to fellow Israelites, but allowed it on loans to foreigners (Dt. 23:20-21, Ev. 23:19-20), while the Holiness Code legislates against interest on loans to the poor in the community (Lev. 25:35-38). Which if any of these texts lies behind Neh. 5:6-13 is impossible to determine. But while the text does not refer to antecedent legislation, there is a hint in v. 9 that the writer is thinking of the Holiness Code. Nehemiah, in reference to the charging of interest, says, "The thing which you are doing is not good. Ought you not to walk in the fear of our God...?" (5:9). The same alternatives are found in Lev.

25:36 (H), which says, "Take no interest from him or increase, but fear your God..." This construction, (do not do this, but fear your God) not found in any of the other texts which deal with loaning at interest, is virtually a refrain in Lev. 25 (H) and occurs elsewhere in the Holiness Code.[99]   Further, like Neh. 5:5-13, Lev. 25:35-55 deals with two issues: charging interest and the enslavement of the poor. Interestingly, the Pentateuch does not forbid the enslavement of the poor, and neither did Nehemiah take any direct action against it. Leviticus 25:39-55 attempts to regulate the practice, that is, it stresses that the fellow Israelite, though a slave, is not to be treated as such and that enslavement is not to be permanent. Slaves can be redeemed or redeem themselves; in any case they are to be freed in the jubilee year. And Nehemiah, although he did not demand that the enslaved poor be freed, appealed to the conscience of the creditors (Neh. 5:8), and struck at the source of the enslavement of the debtors, namely the charging of interest.

The Nehemiah Memoir, as we have seen, received some additions at the end. The first two, Neh. 12:44-47 and 13:1-3, look very much like the Chronicler and may have been composed to connect the Nehemiah Memoir with the rest of the Chronicler's History.[100]   The other two (Neh. 13:15-22 and 23-29), which some scholars regard as original parts of the Memoir,[101] appear less as editorial links to the Chronicler's Work than embellishments of the Nehemiah tradition.[102]   It remains to discuss these texts.

The first, Neh. 12:44-47, refers to "the portions required by the law for the priests and the Levites," but not in such a way that any antecedent legislation can be identified. Verse 47, however, in its reference to the Levites' contribution to the sons of Aaron recalls Num. 18:26-28 (P), the only text in the Hebrew Bible which requires of the Levites that they give to "Aaron the priest" a tithe of the tithe they receive from the people.[103]

Nehemiah 13:1-3 refers to the book of Moses and cites it as the authority for excluding Ammonites and Moabites from the community. The text is a paraphrase of Deut. 23:4-6 (Ev. 23:3-5).

---

[99] Lev. 19:14, 32; 25:17, 36, 43.

[100] Kellermann, *Nehemia*, pp. 47-48; Myers, *Ezra. Nehemiah*, pp. 206-208.

[101] Bowman, *Ezra and Nehemiah*, p. 555. Kellermann, *Nehemia*, pp. 51-55, 57.

[102] Ackroyd, *1 and 2 Chronicles, Ezra, Nehemiah*, p. 314.

[103] Cf. p. 119.

Similarly, in Neh. 13:23-29, although the context lacks a reference to law, written or otherwise, Nehemiah's prohibition of foreign marriages (v. 25), is virtually a quotation of Deut. 7:3.

Finally, Neh. 13:15-22, which describes certain abuses of the Sabbath and Nehemiah's measures to curtail them, makes no reference to the law, and provides no detail by which to determine what specific legislation, if any, was in the writer's mind. It is worth noting, however, that the Pi. of חלל with reference to the Sabbath occurs only in exilic and post-exilic texts.[104]

---

[104] Ex. 31:14 (P); Ezek. 20:13, 16, 21, 24; 22:8; 23:38; Neh. 13:17, 18.

Chapter 6

Conclusion

After the disasters of the early sixth century, the loss of king, land, and independence, the edict of Cyrus in 539 B.C.E. marked the beginning of the Judean restoration and typified what would become the established Persian policy toward captive peoples, their homelands and national religions. We must not underestimate the political insights and intentions which informed this policy, but neither should we underestimate its effects on the history of the Jews. The support of the initial restoration of the community and the temple in Jerusalem as well as the missions of Nehemiah (445 B.C.E.) and Ezra (398 B.C.E.) are manifestations of this Persian policy, and are difficult to comprehend apart from it.

We have seen that the western reaches of the Persian Empire were in the mid-fifth and early-fourth centuries extremely unstable. There were the revolts of Inarus (460 B.C.E.) and Megabyzus (ca. 450 B.C.E.), and by 399 Egypt had gained her independence. Wishing to maintain the western satrapy and fearing that Judah too would seek independence or fall into an Egyptian orbit, the Persian kings (Artaxerxes I and II) took actions which appear to have been benevolent but were in fact expedient: First Nehemiah was sent to restore the walls of Jerusalem, and then Ezra to order the religious life of the community.

Perhaps as a result of these measures Judah did not rebel against Persia or become a vassal to Egypt. But even if their expedient benevolence forestalled a Judean independence movement and thus preserved the peace in Beyond the River, it nevertheless destabilized Judah by furthering what Blenkinsopp has called the tendency to sectarianism.[1]

---

[1] See above pp. 38-39.

Nehemiah did this, as we have seen, by insisting on an exclusive Golah community in Jerusalem and refusing the help even of Yahwistic neighbors. And both Nehemiah and Ezra tried to preserve this purity by forbidding intermarriage with foreigners, which had the effect of dividing the population of Judah; in the reform of Ezra it even divided families and the Golah itself.

Blenkinsopp has identified a major source of this period's sectarian tendency as disagreement on the correct interpretation of authoritative texts and, indeed, on what texts were authoritative.[2] The Chronicler's History, dating from the mid-fourth century, reflects this and is itself a major statement on these questions of interpretation and authority.

We have seen that the Chronicler claimed a book of law available to him to be the authoritative book of the law of Moses. He referred to this book or written law frequently, usually when claiming absolute authority for some cultic practice which was or ought to have been regulated by legislation. Since ancient times this Torah book has been identified as the first part of the Hebrew canon, that is the Torah or Pentateuch.[3]   In modern times this position was argued by Wellhausen[4] and continues to find support.[5]

My analysis of the Chronicler's claims to the authority of written torah and of his descriptions of the requirements of the law book has disclosed at various points a close correspondence between the prescriptions of his Torah book and stipulations contained in the various pentateuchal law codes and sources. It has at the same time, however, raised serious doubts about the thesis that the Chronicler's law book was the Pentateuch.

Predictably, the Chronicler depends primarily on Israel's later legislation, but influences from the ancient law are also occasionally noted. Thus in each of his Passover narratives the Chronicler used

---

[2] Blenkinsopp, "Sectarianism."

[3] b. Baba Bathra 14b-15a; cf. 2 Esdras 14:37-48.

[4] Wellhausen, *Prolegomena*, pp. 405-10.

[5] E.g., Eissfeldt, *The Old Testament*, p. 557; Sellin and Fohrer, *Introduction*, p. 192; Myers, *Ezra. Nehemiah*, pp. 62, 153; Schaeder, *Esra*, pp. 63-64; Cazelles, "La Mission d'Esdras," pp. 113-40; R.J. Coggins, *The Books of Ezra and Nehemiah* (Cambridge, 1976), p. 108; Ackroyd, *1 and 2 Chronicles, Ezra, Nehemiah*, p. 298 (apparently); F. Charles Fensham, *The Books of Ezra and Nehemiah* (Grand Rapids, 1982), p. 105.

the phrase שחט הפסח which occurs elsewhere only at Ex. 12:21 (J).[6]
But in the other instances in which the Chronicler's citations
correspond to the requirements of Israel's earliest codes they also
correspond to more recent legislation which is in agreement with the
ancient practice. An example of this is the sabbatical year release of
crops required by Ex. 23:10 (JE) but also by Lev. 25:1-7 (H).[7]

The Deuteronomic law is more frequently cited, and has had a
greater influence. The Chronicler follows D in naming the three
annual חגים,[8] including Passover which the P legislation had
decentralized,[9] and quotes or paraphrases Deuteronomy three times:
Deut. 24:16 as the reason why the children of Joash's assassins
were not executed with their fathers,[10] Deut. 23:4-6 (Ev. 23:3-5) as
the grounds for the Golah to separate itself from those of foreign
descent,[11] and Deut. 7:3 as the law which forbade mixed
marriages.[12] Finally, only Deuteronomy requires that creditors
forgive outstanding debts in the sabbatical year.[13]

The Chronicler was not constrained, however, by the laws of
Deuteronomy. In addition to his extensive use of priestly legislation
this fact is also demonstrated by the several times that the Chronicler
rejected Deuteronomic torah. An example is his requirement that
הפסח be roasted,[14] but more decisive is his version of the Sukkoth
held by Solomon in conjunction with the dedication of the temple.
The Kings *Vorlage* described an event which conformed to D. The
feast lasted seven days and on the eighth the king sent the people to
their homes.[15] That would have violated the priestly stipulation that
an עצרת be held on the eighth day,[16] however, so the Chronicler
corrected his *Vorlage*. On the eighth day the people held the

---

[6] 2 Chron. 30:15, 17; 35:1, 6, 11; Ezra 6:20.

[7] Neh. 10:32b (Ev. 10:31b).

[8] Deut. 16:1-16, cf. 2 Chron. 8:13.

[9] Ex. 12:1-20.

[10] 2 Chron. 25:4.

[11] Neh. 13:1-3.

[12] Neh. 13:25.

[13] Deut. 15:1-2, cf. Neh. 10:32b (Ev. 10:31b).

[14] 2 Chron. 35:13, cf. Ex. 12:8-9 (P) and Deut. 16:7.

[15] 1 Kgs. 8:65-66.

[16] Lev. 23:36, 39 (H), Num. 29:35 (a supplement to P).

necessary assembly; it was not until the ninth day that the king sent them home.[17]

In addition to this עצרת, the Chronicler's Work follows stipulations found in the Holiness Code for the date of Passover,[18] the relinquishment of crops in the sabbatical year,[19] and perhaps the prohibition of loaning at interest.[20]

More often I have found the Chronicler's descriptions of the Torah book's requirements to correspond to the legislation in P. I have noted the addition to his *Vorlage* of the reason Uzziah got leprosy,[21] the reference to the tax imposed by Moses,[22] and the Chronicler's insistence that the Levites carry the ark.[23] To this may be added the whole range of requirements regarding the payment of tithes and first fruits,[24] including the assignment of all of Israel's tithes to the Levites[25] and the requirement that the Levites in turn pay a tithe of the tithes they receive to the priests.[26] Finally, the delayed celebration of Hezekiah's Passover[27] and the method of cooking הפסח[28] also appear to depend on P.

At other places the requirements of the Chronicler's book of law correspond only to texts which were supplementary to P, some of which may in fact have been included in the Pentateuch after the composition of the Chronicler's History. Examples of this are the list of required occasions for burnt offerings,[29] the instructions for the burning of incense and presentation of the showbread,[30] and

---

[17] 2 Chron. 7:8-10.

[18] Lev. 23:5 (H), cf. 2 Chron. 35:1; Ezra 6:19.

[19] Lev. 25:1-7 (H), but also Ex. 23:10 (JE); cf. Neh. 10:32b (Ev. 10:31b).

[20] Lev. 25:35-38, cf. Neh. 5:6-13 and above, pp. 119-20.

[21] 2 Chron. 26:17-18, cf. 2 Kgs. 15:5, Ex. 30:1-10 (P), Num. 17:5 (Ev. 16:40, P).

[22] 2 Chron. 24:6, cf. Ex. 30:11-16 (P).

[23] 1 Chron. 15:15, cf. 2 Sam. 6, Num. 4:4-15 (P).

[24] Neh. 10:36-38 (Ev. 10:35-37), cf. Num. 18:8-13, 21, 24 (P).

[25] Neh. 13:5, cf. Num. 18:21-24 (P).

[26] Neh. 10:39 (Ev. 10:38), 12:47, cf. Num. 18:26-28 (P).

[27] 2 Chron. 30:15, cf. Num. 9:6-11 (P).

[28] 2 Chron. 35:13, cf. Ex. 12:8-9 (P).

[29] 2 Chron. 31:3, cf. Num. 28-29.

[30] 2 Chron. 2:3 (Ev. 2:4), cf. Ex. 30:1-10, Lev. 24:1-9.

several additions to the Sukkoth ritual, namely: the requirement that the people live in booths,[31] the daily burnt offerings,[32] and the עצרה on the eighth day.[33]

There can no longer be any doubt that the legal material in the Chronicler's History Work assumes a wide range of pentateuchal legislation. What is of equal significance, however, and perhaps even greater interest, is the fact that in several texts the Chronicler attributed to the Torah book legislation not found in the Pentateuch or, indeed, the Hebrew Bible. There is no canonical text to warrant the divorce of foreign wives and the abandonment of one's children borne by them.[34] Neither is there a law that requires a wood offering.[35] Likewise the command to collect branches to make booths ככתוב has not been preserved in the Hebrew Bible.[36] Finally, the organization of priests and Levites,[37] and their roles in the Passover ritual are not based on any legislation now extant.[38] On the other hand, while the evidence is inadequate to show direct dependence, the king's contribution for the burnt offerings and the use of חלל in Pi. of the Sabbath are reminiscent of Ezekiel.[39]

With so rich and variegated a legal tradition to draw upon, it is not surprising that the Chronicler occasionally combined stipulations found previously only in separate collections of law. The requirements for the sabbatical year are an interesting example in that the uniquely Deuteronomic law that debts be forgiven is joined to the command to forego the harvest found in both Ex. 23:10 (JE) and the Holiness code (Lev. 25:1-7) but not in D.[40] This combination of laws, moreover, occurs in a context (Neh. 10:29-39, Ev. 10:28-38)

---

[31] Neh. 8:14, cf. Lev. 23:42.

[32] Ezra 3:4, cf. Num. 29.

[33] Neh. 8:15, cf. Num. 29:35, but also Lev. 23:36, 39 (H).

[34] Ezra 10:3.

[35] Neh. 10:35 (Ev. 10:34). Such a law is, however, an understandable development based on Lev. 6:5-6 (Ev. 6:12-13, P).

[36] Neh. 8:15. Lev. 23:40 (a supplement to P) refers to the *Lulab*; see above, p. 102.

[37] Ezra 6:18.

[38] 2 Chron. 30:16-17; 35:10-11; Ezra 6:20.

[39] 2 Chron. 31:3, cf. Ezek. 45:17; Neh. 13:17, 18, cf. Ezek. 20:13, 16, 21, 24; 22:8; 23:38; but also Ex. 31:14 (P).

[40] Neh. 10:32b (Ev. 10:31b), cf. Deut. 15:1-2.

in which regulations from JE, D, H, and P are all represented and are combined with a reference to a law not found in the Hebrew Bible.[41]

The Chronicler's references to laws and his descriptions of what the written law requires demonstrate that he regarded laws from all of the major pentateuchal codes as authoritative, but depended especially on the later legislative strata. The Chronicler was not limited to pentateuchal legislation, however, since his law book (he claimed) also contained stipulations not found anywhere in the Hebrew Bible. While one must bear in mind that these texts existed in a variety of forms in the Second Temple period, the Chronicler's use of pentateuchal legislation suggests that the exact content of the Torah canon was not yet fixed. His Torah book appears to be more than the canonical Pentateuch,[42] in which case, at least for the Chronicler, the canonization of the Torah had not yet occurred.

---

[41] The sabbatical year release of crops is found in JE (Ex. 23:10) and H (Lev. 25:1-7), the sabbatical year forgiveness of debts in D (Deut. 15:1-2), the prohibition of marriage to foreigners in D (Deut. 7:3), and the laws on first fruits and tithes in P (Num. 18:8-29). The wood offering is not found in the Hebrew Bible.

[42] Some have suggested that the Chronicler's Torah book was *less* than the canonical Pentateuch. This has been argued on the basis that Neh. 8, which narrates the reading of the law on the first day of the seventh month and a subsequent feast of Sukkoth, makes no mention of the great fast day, *Yom Kippur*, which H (Lev. 23:27-32) and P (Lev. 16:29-34) dated on the tenth day of the seventh month, cf. Smith *Palestinian Parties*, pp. 123, 273, and Blenkinsopp, "Sectarianism," p. 6. I have noted above (p. 84, n. 20) that the dates in H and P may be additions to their contexts and that Neh. 9:1-5 may refer to *Yom Kippur*. On the other hand, one must be wary of arguments from silence. The Chronicler was selective and eclectic in his use of antecedent legislation; he did not always follow P (cf., e.g., Passover as a חג), and the fact that he makes no reference to a pentateuchal law, or even contradicts it, does not require the view that the law did not exist or even that the Chronicler was ignorant of it.

Chronological Table

Cyrus, 550-530
    The edict of Cyrus, 539
    Initial return of some Jews
    Sheshbazzar
    The rebuilding of the altar (?), ca. 535

Cambyses, 530-522
    Persian conquest of Egypt , 525

Darius I, 522-486
    Zerubbabel
    The rebuilding of the temple, 520-515

Xerxes I, 486-465

Artaxerxes I, 465-424
    The revolt of Inarus, 460
    The revolt of Megabyzus, ca. 450
    The mission of Nehemiah, 445-433
    Sanballat I

Xerxes II, 423

Darius II, 423-404
    Temple of Yahu at Elephantine destroyed, 410

Artaxerxes II, 404-358
    The founding of the independent twenty-ninth
        Egyptian dynasty, 399
    The mission of Ezra, 398 (or 458)

Bibliography

Ackroyd, Peter R. "The Chronicler as Exegete," *Journal for the Study of the Old Testament*, II (1977), 2-32.

_____. "Chronicles I and II," *The Interpreter's Dictionary of the Bible*, Supplementary Vol. (1976), 156-58.

_____. *1 and 2 Chronicles, Ezra, and Nehemiah: Introduction and Commentary*. Torch Bible Commentary. London: S.C.M. Press, 1973.

_____. *Exile and Restoration: A Study of Hebrew Thought of the Sixth Century B.C.* The Old Testament Library, London: S.C.M. Press, 1968.

_____. "History and Theology in the Writings of the Chronicler," *Concordia Theological Monthy*, XXXVIII (1967), 501-15.

_____. "Israel in the Exilic and Post-Exilic Periods." In *Tradition and Interpretation*, pp. 320-50. Edited by George W. Anderson. Oxford: Clarendon Press, 1979.

_____. *Israel Under Babylon and Persia*. The New Clarendon Bible, Old Testament, IV. Oxford: Oxford University Press, 1970.

_____. "Original Text and Canonical Text," *Union Seminary Quarterly Review*, XXXII (1976), 166-73.

_____. "The Theology of the Chronicler," *Lexington Theological Quarterly*, VIII (1973), 101-16.

_____. "Two Old Testament Historical Problems of the Early Persian Period," *Journal of Near Eastern Studies*, XVII (1958), 13-27.

Albright, William F. *The Biblical Period from Abraham to Ezra.* Revised and expanded ed. New York: Harper & Row, 1963.

_____. "The Date and Personality of the Chronicler," *Journal of Biblical Literature*, XL (1921), 104-24.

Allen, Leslie C. *The Greek Chronicles: The Relationship of the Septuagint of I and II Chronicles to the Massoretic text.* Leiden: E.J. Brill, 1974.

Anderson, George W. *A Critical Instroduction to the Old Testament.* London: G. Duckworth, 1959.

_____. "Some Aspects of the Uppsala School of Old Testament Study," *Harvard Theological Review*, XVIII (1950), 239-56.

Auerbach, Elias. "Die Feste im alten Israel," *Vetus Testamentum*, VIII (1958), 1-18.

Batten, Loring W. *A Critical and Exegetical Commentary on the Books of Ezra and Nehemiah.* The International Critical Commentary. Edinburgh: T. & T. Clark, 1913.

Bentzen, A. "Sirach, der Chronist und Nehemia," *Studia Theologica*, III (1949), 158-61.

Bertholet, A. *Die Bücher Esra und Nehemia.* Tübingen: J.C.B. Mohr, 1902.

Bickermann, Elias. "The Edict of Cyrus in Ezra I," *Journal of Biblical Literature*, LXV (1946), 249-75.

_____. *From Ezra to the Last of the Maccabees.* New York: Schocken Books, 1962.

Blenkinsopp, Joseph. "Interpretation and the Tendency to Sectarianism: An Aspect of Second Temple History." In

Jewish and Christian Self-Definition, II: Two Aspects of Judaism in the Greco-Roman Period, pp. 1-26. Edited by Edward P. Sanders, *et al.* Philadelphia: Fortress Press, 1981.

_____. *Prophecy and Canon.* Notre Dame and London: University of Notre Dame Press, 1977.

Bossmann, David. "Ezra's Marriage Reform: Israel Redefined," *Biblical Theology Bulletin*, IX (1979), 32-38.

Botterweck, C.J. "Zur Eigenart der Chronistischen Davidgeschichte," *Theologische Quartalschrift*, CXXXVI (1956), 402-34.

Bowman, Raymond A. *Introduction and Exegesis to the Book of Ezra and the Book of Nehemiah.* The Interpreter's Bible, III, 547-819. New York and Nashville: Abingdon Press, 1954.

Braun, Roddy L. "Chronicles, Ezra, and Nehemiah: Theology and Literary History." In *Studies in the Historical Books of the Old Testament.* Edited by J.A. Emerton. Supplements to *Vetus Testamentum*, XXX. Leiden: E.J. Brill, 1979.

_____. "The Message of Chronicles: Rally Round the Temple," *Concordia Theological Monthly*, XLII (1971), 502-14.

_____. "Solomonic Apologetic in Chronicles," *Journal of Biblical Literature*, XCII (1973), 503-16.

Bright, John. "The Date of Ezra's Mission to Jerusalem." In *Yehezkel Kaufmann Jubilee Volume*, pp. 70-87. Edited by M. Haran. Jerusalem: Magnes Press, 1960.

_____. *A History of Israel.* 2nd ed. London: S.C.M. Press, 1972.

Brockington, Leonard H. *Ezra, Nehemiah and Esther.* The Century Bible, New Series. London: Nelson, 1969.

Brown, F., Driver, S. R. and Briggs, C. A. *A Hebrew and English Lexicon of the Old Testament*. Oxford: Clarendon Press, 1907.

Brunet, A.M. "Le Chroniste et ses Sources," *Revue Biblique*, LX (1953), 481-508 and LXI (1954), 349-86.

Burn, Andrew R. *Persia and the Greeks: The Defense of the West, c. 546-478 B.C.* New York: St. Martin's Press, 1962.

Cancik, H. "Das jüdische Fest. Ein Versuch zu Form und Religion des Chronistischen Geschichtswerks," *Theologische Quartalschrift*, CL (1970), 335-48.

Cazelles, Henri. *Les Livres des Chroniques*. La Sainte Bible. Paris: Les Editions du Cerf, 1954.

_____. "La mission d'Esdras," *Vetus Testamentum*, IV (1954), 113-40.

Childs, Brevard S. *Biblical Theology in Crisis*. Philadelphia: Westminster Press, 1970.

Clements, Ronald. *One Hundred Years of Old Testament Interpretation*. Philadelphia: Westminster Press, 1976.

_____. "Pentateuchal Problems." In *Tradition and Interpretation*, pp. 96-124. Edited by George W. Anderson. Oxford: Clarendon Press, 1979.

Coats, George W. and Long, Burke O. (eds.). *Canon and Authority*. Philadelphia: Fortress Press, 1977.

Coggins, R.J. *The Books of Ezra and Nehemiah*. Cambridge Bible Commentary. London and New York: Cambridge University Press, 1976.

_____. *The First and Second Books of the Chronicles*. Cambridge Bible Commentary. London and New York: Cambridge University Press, 1976.

_____. "The Interpretation of Ezra IV:4," *Journal of Theological Studies*, ns XIV (1965), 124-27.

_____. *Samaritans and Jews: The Origins of Samaritanism Reconsidered.* Oxford: Blackwell, 1975.

Cook, J.M. *The Persian Empire.* London: J.M. Dent & Sons, 1983.

Cook, S.A. "The Age of Zerubbabel." In *Studies in Old Testament Prophecy*, pp. 19-36. Edited by Harold H. Rowley. Edinburgh: T. & T. Clark, 1950.

Cowley, A. *Aramaic Papyri of the Fifth Century B.C.* Oxford: Clarendon Press, 1923.

Cross, Frank Moore. "Aspects of Samaritan and Jewish History in Late Persian Times," *Harvard Theological Review*, LIX (1966), 201-11.

_____. "The Discovery of the Samaria Papyri," *The Biblical Archaeologist*, XXVI (1963), 110-21.

_____. "Papyri of the Fourth Century from Dâliyeh." In *New Directions in Biblical Archeology*, pp. 41-61. Edited by David Noel Freedman and J. Greenfield. New York: Doubleday, 1969.

_____. "A Reconstruction of the Judean Restoration," *Journal of Biblical Literature*, XCIV (1975), 4-18.

Cross, Frank Moore and Talmon, Shemaryahu (eds.). *Qumran and the History of the Biblical Text.* Cambridge: Harvard University Press, 1975.

Curtis, Edward Lewis, and Madsen, Albert Alonzo. *A Critical and Exegetical Commentary on the Books of Chronicles.* The International Critical Commentary. Edinburgh: T. & T. Clark, 1910.

de Vaux, Roland. *Ancient Israel: Its Life and Institutions.* 2 vols. Translated by John McHugh. London: Darton, Longman and Todd, 1961.

Driver, Samuel Rolles. *A Critical and Exegetical Commentary on Deuteronomy*. The International Critical Commentary. New York: Charles Scribner's Sons, 1895.

_____. *An Introduction to the Literature of the Old Testament*. Gloucester: Peter Smith, 1972.

Eissfeldt, Otto. *The Old Testament: An Introduction*. Translated by Peter R. Ackroyd. New York: Harper and Row, 1965.

Elmslie, W.A.L. *The First and Second Books of Chronicles*. The Interpreter's Bible, III, 339-548. New York and Nashville: Abingdon Press, 1954.

Emerton, J.H. "Did Ezra go to Jersualem in 428 B.C.?" *Journal of Theological Studies*, XVII (1966), 1-19.

Fensham, F. Charles. *The Books of Ezra and Nehemiah*. Grand Rapids: Eerdmans, 1982.

Fohrer, Georg. *History of Israelite Religion*. Translated by David E. Green. Nashville and New York: Abingdon Press, 1972.

Freedman, David Noel. "The Chronicler's Purpose," *Catholic Biblical Quarterly*, XXIII (1961), 436-42.

Galling, Kurt. *Die Bücher der Chronik, Esra, Nehemia*. Das Alte Testament Deutsch. Göttingen: Vandenhoeck & Ruprect, 1954.

_____. "The Gola-List According to Ezra 2 // Nehemiah 7," *Journal of Biblical Literature*, LXX (1951), 149-58.

_____. *Studien zur Geschichte Israels im persischen Zeitalter*. Tübingen: J.C.B. Mohr, 1964.

Gaster, M. "The Feast of Jeroboam and the Samaritan Calendar," *Expository Times*, XXIV (1913), 198-201.

Gelin, A. *Le Livre de Esdras et Néhémie*. 2nd ed. La Sainte Bible. Paris: Les Editions du Cerf, 1960.

Ginsberg, H.L. "Ezra 1:4," *Journal of Biblical Literature*, LXXIX (1960), 167-69.

Gray, G. Buchanan. "The Foundation and Extension of the Persian Empire." In *The Cambridge Ancient History, IV, The Persian Empire and the West*, pp. 1-25. Edited by J.B. Bury, S.A. Cook and F.E. Adcock. Cambridge: Cambridge University Press, 1926.

_____. "Passover and Unleavened Bread, The Laws of J, E, and D," *Journal of Theological Studies*, XXXVII (1936), 241-53.

Herrmann, Siegfried. *A History of Israel in Old Testament Times*. 2nd ed. Translated by John Bowden. Philadelphia: Fortress Press, 1981.

Howorth, H.H. "The Real Character and the Importance of the First Book of Esdras, II," *The Academy*, XLIII (1893), 60.

in der Smitten, Wilhelm Th. *Esra. Quellen, Überlieferung und Geschichte*. Studia Semitic Nearlandica, XV. Assen: Van Gorcum, 1973.

_____. "Die Gründe für die Aufnahme der Nehemiaschrift in das Chronistische Geschichtswerk," *Biblische Zeitschrift*, XVI (1972), 207-21.

Japhet, Sara. "Chronicles, Book of," *Encyclopaedia Judaica*, V (1971), cols. 517-34.

_____. "Conquest and Settlement in Chronicles," *Journal of Biblical Literature*, XCVIII (1979), 205-18.

_____. "The Supposed Common Authorship of Chronicles and Ezra-Nehemiah Investigated Anew," *Vetus Testamentum*, XVIII (1968), 330-71.

Jellicoe, Sidney. "Nehemiah--Ezra: A Reconstruction," *Expositary Times*, LIX (1947-48), 54.

Jepson, A. "Nehemiah 10," *Zeitschrift für die alttestamentliche Wissenschaft*, LXVI (1954), 87-106.

Johnson, M.D. *The Purpose of the Biblical Genealogies.* Society for New Testament Studies Monograph Series, VIII. Cambridge: Cambridge University Press, 1969.

Josephus. *Jewish Antiquities*, Books IX-XI. The Loeb Classical Library, No. 326. Translated by Ralph Marcus. Cambridge: Harvard University Press, 1937.

Kahle, Paul. *The Cairo Geniza.* London: Oxford University Press, 1947.

Kapelrud, Arvid S. *The Question of Authorship in the Ezra Narrative. A Lexical Investigation.* Skifter utgitt av Det Norske Videnskaps-Akademi i Oslo, II, Hist. -Filos. Klasse. No. 1. Oslo: J. Dybwad, 1944.

Kegel, M. *Die Kultusreformation des Esra.* Gütersloh: Berteismann, 1921.

Kellermann, Ulrich. "Erwägungen zum Esragesetz," *Zeitschrift für die alttestamentliche Wissenschaft*, LXXX (1968), 373-85.

_____. "Erwägungen zum Problem der Esradatierung," *Zeitschrift für die alttestamentliche Wissenschaft*, LXXX (1968), 55-87.

_____. *Nehemia: Quellen, Überlieferung und Geschichte.* Beihefte zur *Zeitschrift für die alttestamentliche Wissenschaft*, CII. Berlin: Verlag Alfred Töpelmann, 1967.

Klein, Ralph W. "Ezra and Nehemiah in Recent Studies." In *Magnalia Dei, The Mightly Acts of God*, pp. 361-76. Edited by Frank Moore Cross, *et al.* Garden City: Doubleday, 1976.

_____. "Jeroboam's Rise to Power," *Journal of Biblical Literature*, LXXXIX (1970), 217-18.

_____. "Once More: Jeroboam's Rise to Power," *Journal of Biblical Literature*, XCII (1973), 582-84.

Kock, Klaus. "Ezra and the Origins of Judaism," *Journal of Semitic Studies*, XIX (1974), 173-97.

Kraeling, Emil G. *The Brooklyn Museum Aramaic Papyri. New Documents of the Fifth Century B.C. from the Jewish Colony at Elephantine.* New Haven: Yale University Press, 1953.

Kraus, Hans-Joachim. *Geschichte der historisch-kritischen Erforschung des Alten Testaments.* 2. Aufl. Neukirchen-Vluyn: Neukrichener Verlag, 1969.

_____. *Worship in Israel.* Translated by Geoffrey Busswell. Oxford: Blackwell, 1966.

_____. "Zur Geschichte des Passah--Massot Festes im alten Testament," *Evangelische Theologie,* XVIII (1958), 47-67.

Leeseberg, M.W. "Ezra and Nehemiah: A Review of the Return and Reform," *Concordia Theological Monthly,* XXXIII (1962), 79-90.

Lemke, Werner E. "The Synoptic Problem in the Chronicler's History," *Harvard Theological Review,* LVIII (1965), 349-63.

Mantel, H.D. "The Dichotomy of Judaism During the Second Temple," *Hebrew Union College Annual,* XLIV (1973), 55-87.

May, H.G. "The Relation of the Passover to the Festival of Unleavened Cakes," *Journal of Biblical Literature,* LV (1936), 65-82.

Milik, Józef. *Ten Years of Discovery in the Wilderness of Judaea.* Translated by J. Strugnell. Naperville: A.R. Allenson, 1959.

Morgenstern, J. "The Dates of Ezra and Nehemiah," *Journal of Semitic Studies,* VII (1962), 1-11.

Moriarty, F.L. "The Chronicler's Account of Hezekiah's Reform," *Catholic Biblical Quarterly,* XXVII (1965), 399-406.

Mosis, Rudolf. *Untersuchen zur Theologie des chronistischen Geschichtswerkes.* Freiburger theologische Studien, XCII. Freiburg: Herder, 1973.

Mowinckel, Sigmund. "Erwägungen zum chronistischen Geschichtswerk," *Theologische Literaturzeitung,* LXXXV (1965), 1-8.

_____. *Studien zu dem Buche Ezra--Nehemia I: Die nachchronistische Redaktion des Buches. Die Listen.* Skrifter utgitt av Det Norske Videnskaps-Akademi i Oslo, II, Hist. Filos. Klasse. No. 3. Oslo: J. Dybwad, 1944.

_____. *Studien zu dem Buche Ezra--Nehemia II: Die Nehemia--Denkschrift.* Skrifter utgitt av Det Norske Videnskaps-Akademi i Oslo, II, Hist. -Filos. Klasse. No. 5. Oslo: J. Dybwad, 1964.

_____. *Studien zu dem Buche Ezra--Nehemia III: Die Ezrageschichte und das Gesetz Moses.* Skrifter utgitt av Det Norske Videnskaps-Akademi i Oslo, II, Hist. -Filos. Klasse. No. 7. Oslo: J. Dybwad, 1965.

Myers, Jacob M. *I Chronicles. Introduction, Translation, and Notes.* The Anchor Bible, XII. Garden City: Doubleday, 1965.

_____. *II Chronicles. Introduction, Translation, and Notes.* The Anchor Bible, XIII. Garden City: Doubleday, 1965.

_____. *I and II Esdras. Introduction, Translation, and Commentary.* The Anchor Bible, XLII. Garden City: Doubleday, 1974.

_____. *Ezra. Nehemiah. Introduction, Translation, and Notes.* The Anchor Bible, XIV. Garden City: Doubleday, 1965.

_____. "The Kerygma of the Chronicler," *Interpretation,* XX (1966), 259-73.

_____. *The World of the Restoration.* Englewood Cliffs: Prentice-Hall, 1968.

Neufeld, E. "The Rate of Interest and the Text of Nehemiah 5:11," *Jewish Quarterly Review*, XLIV (1953-54), 194-204.

Newsome, J.D. "Toward a New Understanding of the Chronicler and His Purposes," *Journal of Biblical Literature*, XCIV (1975), 201-17.

North, C.R. *The Old Testament Interpretation of History.* London: The Epworth Press, 1946.

_____. "Pentateuchal Criticism." In *The Old Testament and Modern Study*, pp. 48-83. Edited by Harold H. Rowley. Oxford: Clarendon Press, 1951.

North, Robert. "The Theology of the Chronicler," *Journal of Biblical Literature*, LXXXII (1963), 369-86.

Noth, Martin. *Exodus: A Commentary.* The Old Testament Library. Translated by J.S. Bowden. Philadelphia: Westminster Press, 1962.

_____. *The History of Israel.* 2nd ed. Translated by Peter R. Ackroyd. New York: Harper & Row, 1960.

_____. *A History of Pentateuchal Traditions.* Translated by Bernhard W. Anderson. Englewood Cliffs: Prentice-Hall, 1972.

_____. *Leviticus: A Commentary.* Revised ed. The Old Testament Library. Translated by J.E. Anderson. Philadelphia: Westminster Press, 1977.

_____. *Numbers: A Commentary.* The Old Testament Library. Translated by James D. Martin. Philadelphia: Westminster Press, 1968.

_____. *The Old Testament World.* Translated by Victor I. Gruhn. Philadelphia: Fortress Press, 1966.

_____. *Überlieferungsgeschichtliche Studien I.* 3rd ed. Tübingen: Max Niemeyer, 1967.

Olmstead, Albert T. *History of Palestine and Syria to the Macedonian Conquest.* New York and London: Charles Scribners' Sons, 1931.

_____. *History of the Persian Empire.* Chicago: University of Chicago Press, 1948.

Pfeiffer, Robert H. "Chronicles, 1 and 2," *The Interpreter's Dictionary of the Bible,* I (1962), 572-80.

_____. *Introduction to the Old Testament.* New York: Harper & Row, 1948.

Pohlmann, Karl-Friedrich. *Studien zum Dritten Esra. Ein Beitrag zur Frage nach dem Ursprünglich Schluss des Chronistischen Geschichtswerks.* Göttingen: Vandenhoeck u. Ruprecht, 1970.

Porter, J.R. "Son or Grandson (Ezra 10:6)?" *Journal of Theological Studies,* ns XVII (1966), 54-67.

Pritchard, James B. (ed.). *Ancient Near Eastern Texts Relating to the Old Testament.* Princeton: Princeton University Press, 1950.

Rowley, Harold H. "The Chronological Order of Ezra and Nehemiah." In *The Servant of the Lord and Other Essays on the Old Testament.* 2nd ed. pp. 137-68. Oxford: Blackwell, 1965.

_____. "Nehemiah's Mission and its Background," *Bulletin of the John Rylands Library,* XXXVII (1955), 528-61.

_____. "Sanballat and the Samaritan Temple," *Bulletin of the John Rylands Library,* XXXVIII (1956), 166-98.

Rudolph, Wilhelm. *Chronikbücher.* Handbuch zum Alten Testament. Tübingen: J.C.B. Mohr, 1955.

_____. *Esra und Nehemia mit 3. Esra.* Handbuch zum Alten Testament. Tübingen: J.C.B. Mohr, 1949.

_____. "Problems with the Books of Chronicles," *Vetus Testamentum*, IV (1954), 401-409.

Saley, Richard J. "The Date of Nehemiah Reconsidered." In *Biblical and Near Eastern Studies: Essays in Honor of William Sanford LaSor*, pp. 151-65. Edited by G.A. Tuttle. Grand Rapids: Eerdmans, 1978.

Sanders, James A. "Adaptable for Life: The Nature and Function of Canon." In *Magnalia Dei, The Mighty Acts of God*, pp. 531-60. Edited by Frank Moore Cross, et al. Garden City: Doubleday, 1976.

_____. *Torah and Canon.* Philadelphia: Fortress Press, 1972.

Schaeder, H.H. *Esra der Schreiber.* Beiträge zur historischen Theologie, V. Tübingen: J.C.B. Mohr, 1930.

Schneider, H. *Die Bücher Esra und Nehemia.* Die Heilige Schrift des Alten Testaments. Bonn: Peter Hanstein Verlag, 1959.

Segal, Judah B. *The Hebrew Passover: From the Earliest Times to A.D. 70.* London Oriental Series, XII. London and New York: Oxford University Press, 1963.

Sellin, Ernst and Fohrer, Georg. *Introduction to the Old Testament.* Translated by David E. Green. Nashville and New York: Abindgon Press, 1968.

Smend, Rudolph. *Die Entstehung des Alten Testaments.* Stuttgart: Kohlhammer, 1978.

Smith, Morton. *Palestinian Parties and Politics that Shaped the Old Testament.* New York: Columbia University Press, 1971.

Snaith, Norman H. "The Date of Ezra's Arrival in Jerusalem," *Zeitschrift für die alttestamentliche Wissenschaft*, LXVIII (1951), 53-66.

_____. "The Historical Books." In *The Old Testament and Modern Study*, pp. 84-114. Edited by Harold H. Rowley. Oxford: Clarendon Press, 1951.

Soggin, J. Alberto. *Introduction to the Old Testament*. The Old Testament Library. Translated by John Bowden. Philadelphia: Westminster Press, 1976.

Swanson, Theodore N. "The Closing of the Collection of Holy Scriptures: A Study in the History of the Canonization of the Old Testament." Unpublished doctoral dissertation. Religion Department, Vanderbilt University, 1970.

Talmon, Shemaryahu. "Divergencies in Calendar Reckoning in Ephraim and Judah," *Vetus Testamentum*, VIII (1958), 48-74.

Torrey, Charles Cutler. "The Aramaic Portions of Ezra," *American Journal of Semitic Languages and Literature*, XXIV (1907-08), 209-81.

_____. "The Chronicler as Editor and as Independent Narrator," *American Journal of Semitic Languages and Literatures*, XXV (1908-09), 157-73, 188-217.

_____. *The Chronicler's History of Israel*. New Haven: Yale University Press, 1954.

_____. *Composition and Historical Value of Ezra--Nehemiah*. Beihefte zur *Zeitschrift für die alttestamentliche Wissenschaft*, II. Berlin: Verlag Alfred Töpelmann, 1896.

_____. *Ezra Studies*. Chicago: Chicago University Press, 1910.

Tuland, Carl G. "Ezra-Nehemiah or Nehemiah-Ezra?," *Andrews University Seminary Studies*, XII/1 (1974), 47-62.

_____. "Josephus, *Antiquities*, Book XI. Correction or Confirmation of Biblical Post-Exilic Records?," *Andrews University Seminary Studies*, IV (1966), 176-92.

Ulrich, Eugene Charles. *The Qumran Text of Samuel and Josephus*. Harvard Semitic Monographs, XIX. Missoula: Scholars Press, 1978.

von Rad, Gerhard. *Deuteronomy: A Commentary*. The Old Testament Library. Translated by Dorothea Barton. London: S.C.M. Press, 1966.

_____. "The Form Critical Problem of the Hexateuch." In *The Problem of the Hexateuch and Other Essays*, pp. 1-78. Translated by E.W. Trueman Dicken. New York: McGraw Hill, 1966.

_____. *Das Geschichtsbild des Chronistischen Werkes*. Stuttgart: Kohlhammer, 1930.

_____. "The Levitical Sermon in I & II Chronicles." In *The Problem of the Hexateuch and Other Essays*, pp. 267-80. Translated by E.W. Trueman Dicken. New York: McGraw Hill, 1966.

Wagner, N.E. "Pentateuchal Criticism: No Clear Future," *Canadian Journal of Theology*, XIII (1967), 225-32.

Walde, Bernhard. *Die Esdrasbücher der Septuaginta*. Freiburg: Herder, 1913.

Weiser, Artur. *The Old Testament: Its Formation and Development*. Translated by Dorothea Barton. New York: Association Press, 1961.

Welch, Adam C. "On the Method of Celebrating Passover," *Zeitschrift für die alttestamentliche Wissenschaft*, XLV (1927), 24-29.

_____. *Post-Exilic Judaism*. Edinburgh and London: Blackwood, 1935.

_____. *The Work of the Chronicler: Its Purpose and Its Date*. London: Oxford University Press, 1939.

Wellhausen, Julius. *Prolegomena to the History of Israel.* Translated by J. Sutherland Black and Allan Menzies. New York: Meridian Books, 1957.

Welten, Peter. *Geschichte und Geschichtsdarstellung in den Chronikbüchern.* Neukirchen-Vluyn: Neukirchener Verlag, 1973.

Widengren, Geo. "The Persian Period." In *Israelite and Judean History*, pp. 489-538. Edited by John H. Hayes and J. Maxwell Miller. Philadelphia: Westminster Press, 1977.

Willi, Thomas. *Die Chronik als Auslegung; Untersuchungen zur literarischen Gestaltung der historischen Überlieferung Israels.* Göttingen: Vandenhoeck u. Ruprecht, 1972.

_____. "Thora in den biblischen Chronikbüchern," *Judaica*, XXXVI (1980), 102-105, 148-51.

Williamson, H.G.M. *1 and 2 Chronicles.* The New Century Bible Commentary. Grand Rapids and London: Eerdmans and Marshall, Morgan & Scott, 1982.

_____. *Israel in the Books of Chronicles.* Cambridge: Cambridge University Press, 1977.

Wiseman, D.J. "Books in the Ancient Near East and in the Old Testament." In *The Cambridge History of the Bible, I, From the Beginnings to Jerome*, pp. 30-48. Edited by Peter R. Ackroyd and C.F. Evans. Cambridge: Cambridge University Press, 1970.

Wright, J.S. *The Date of Ezra's Coming to Jerusalem.* London: Tyndale Press, 1958.

Zunz, Leopold A. *Die gottesdienstlichen Vorträge der Juden, historisch entwickelt. Ein Beitrag zur Alterthumskunde und biblischen Kritik, zur Literatur- und Religionsgeschichte.* Berlin: A. Asher, 1832.

Index of Passages

Index of Modern Authors

www.ingramcontent.com/pod-product-compliance
Lightning Source LLC
Chambersburg PA
CBHW022023090426
42739CB00006BA/260